DATE DUE

JAN 3 1 2004			
MAR 0 7			
GAYLORD			PRINTED IN U.S.A.

FRIEDRICH A. SORGE'S
Labor Movement
in the United States

Recent Titles in
Contributions in Economics and Economic History
Series Editor: Robert Sobel

Moving and Shaking American Medicine: The Structure of a Socioeconomic Transformation
Betty Leyerle

The Age of Giant Corporations: A Microeconomic History of American Business, 1914-1984; A Second Edition
Robert Sobel

The Antimonopoly Persuasion: Popular Resistance to the Rise of Big Business in the Midwest
Steven L. Piott

Working the Range: Essays on the History of Western Land Management and the Environment
John R. Wunder, editor

Off the Track: The Decline of the Intercity Passenger Train in the United States
Donald M. Itzkoff

The Crash and Its Aftermath: A History of Securities Markets in the United States, 1929-1933
Barrie A. Wigmore

Synthetic Rubber: A Project That Had to Succeed
Vernon Herbert and Attilio Bisio

Military Spending and Industrial Decline: A Study of the American Machine Tool Industry
Anthony Di Filippo

Famine in Peasant Societies
Ronald E. Seavoy

Workforce Management in the Arabian Peninsula: Forces Affecting Development
George S. Roukis and Patrick J. Montana, editors

A Prologue to National Development Planning
Jamshid Gharajedaghi

Lost Initiatives: Canada's Forest Industries, Forest Policy and Forest Conservation
R. Peter Gillis and Thomas R. Roach

FRIEDRICH A. SORGE'S
Labor Movement in the United States

A History of the American Working Class
from 1890 to 1896

Translated by KAI SCHOENHALS

Contributions in Economics and Economic History, Number 73

Greenwood Press
New York • Westport, Connecticut • London

Library of Congress Cataloging-in-Publication Data

Sorge, Friedrich A. (Friedrich Adolf), 1828-1906.
  Friedrich A. Sorge's labor movement in the United
States.

  (Contributions in economics and economic history,
ISSN 0084-9235 ; no. 73)
  Bibliography: p.
  Includes Index.
  1. Labor and laboring classes—United States—
History—19th century. 2. Labor disputes—United
States—History—19th century. 3. Trade-unions—
United States—History—19th century. I. Schoenhals,
Kai P. II. Title. III. Title: Labor movement in the
United States. IV. Series.
HD8072.S7175 1987   331'.0973   86-31792
ISBN 0-313-25518-0 (lib. bdg. : alk. paper)

Library of Congress Catalog Card Number: 86-31792
ISBN: 0-313-25518-0
ISSN: 0084-9235

First published in 1987

Greenwood Press, Inc.
88 Post Road West, Westport, Connecticut 06881

Printed in the United States of America

∞

The paper used in this book complies with the
Permanent Paper Standard issued by the National
Information Standards Organization (Z39.48-1984).

10 9 8 7 6 5 4 3 2 1

TO MY MOTHER

ANNELIESE BORN-SCHOENHALS

WITH LOVE AND ADMIRATION

Contents

viii   Contents

Introduction
by Kai Schoenhals

In 1977, Greenwood Press published some of the articles which Friedrich A. Sorge, the German-American Marxist, had written between 1891 and 1896 for <u>Die Neue Zeit</u>, the theoretical journal of the Social Democratic Party of Germany. These articles, collectively entitled <u>The Labor Movement in the United States</u>, covered the history of the American working class from colonial times until 1890. The translation of the German text had been arranged by Angela and Brewster Chamberlin, while a preface and an extensive biographical account of Sorge was provided by Philip S. Foner. Although Sorge had formally concluded his history of the American labor movement with the year 1890, he wrote enough additional material between 1892 and the end of the century to warrant a second volume.

A few years ago, I was asked to translate the second volume. Unfortunately, Foner wasn't able to write an introduction for this volume, as he had hoped he could, and I am reluctantly writing it myself in order to make the translation of Sorge's second volume available to an English-speaking audience. The translation should be made available because Sorge happened to be one of the pioneers of modern American socialism.

Friedrich Adolph Sorge (1828-1906) was born in Germany, in a small hamlet near Torgau on the Elbe River, where American and Soviet soldiers later joined forces at the end of World War II. His father was a liberal Protestant minister who provided his son Friedrich with a good education, particularly in the field of music. The year 1848 found the Sorges on the losing side of the revolution. Friedrich A. Sorge, as a matter of fact, fought in the ultimate engagement of the revolutionary forces in Baden (June 1849) alongside Friedrich Engels. Then came exile in Switzerland, Belgium, and England. Condemned to death in his native

Prussia, Sorge decided to leave Europe permanently. He
arrived in New York during 1852. Little is known about
his first decade in the United States, except that he
could barely eke out a living as a music teacher. Like
so many "forty-eighters," he did not for a long time
give up the hope that his native land would eventually
be united under a liberal democratic government.
Instead came the unification of Germany by Bismarck,
the Hohenzollern and Reaction.

Sorge found himself drawn into radical labor
politics upon his arrival in the United States, but it
was not until after the American Civil War that he
embraced Marxism. In 1867 Sorge asked Karl Marx for
permission to set up a branch of the International
Workingmen's Association (IWA) in the United States, a
request to which Marx responded enthusiastically.
Sorge was to correspond with the founder of scientific
socialism until the latter's death in 1883. In 1869,
Section I of the IWA was founded at Hoboken, New Jersey,
with Sorge becoming its president and secretary.

By 1872 the IWA in Europe found itself threatened
by both persecution and desertion because of the wide-
spread belief that it had been instrumental in
organizing the Paris Commune of 1871. Its continued
existence was further imperiled by the intense struggle
for leadership between the Socialists and the Anarchists.
At the IWA's Hague Congress of 1872, it was decided to
move the headquarters of the IWA General Council to the
calmer atmosphere of New York. As America's leading
Marxist at the Hague Congress, Sorge was elected as the
general secretary of the IWA's General Council.

Upon his return to America, Sorge faced the
formidable task of holding the IWA together. Not only
were the resources of that organization thoroughly
depleted, but the depression of 1873 dealt an additional
blow to its precarious financial state. Even more
threatening to its survival was the bitter struggle
between the followers of Lassalle and Marx. The
Lassalleans believed that trade unions were of little
value since workers' pay, determined by the "Iron Law
of Wages," would always be kept at a minimum level.
The Lassalleans, therefore, urged the workers to break
out of this hopeless situation by becoming involved in
politics. The achievement of electoral victories would
eventually lead to the establishment of their own
cooperatives, which the Lassalleans regarded as the
ultimate panacea. In contrast, Marxists such as Sorge
believed that workers should first concentrate on
forming strong labor unions in order to wring concessions (such as the eight hour day, the right to
strike, etc.) from their bosses before becoming
embroiled in politics. As a consequence of this bitter
factional strife, Sorge was ousted from the General

Council of the IWA in 1874. Two years later the
moribund IWA was officially dissolved.
    Shortly after the IWA's demise, there were hopeful
signs that the Lassalleans and Marxists would reconcile
their differences in order to form a common front
against the capitalist enemies. Inspired by the Gotha
Unity Congress (1875), which had resulted in the formation of a united Social Democratic Party in Germany,
American Socialists of various shades formed in 1876
the first unified Socialist party in the United States.
This Workingmen's Party of the United States was Marxist
in orientation largely because of the efforts of Sorge
whose hopes for an eventual Socialist victory in America
were buoyed by this development. However, shortly
after the formation of this unity party, the bitter
rivalry between Lassalleans and Marxists erupted anew
and the Lassalleans were able to transform the party and
its press organs to their viewpoint, eliminating all
Marxist influence in the process. By 1877 Sorge and the
other Marxist members had resigned from the party,
which by then had changed its name to the Socialist
Labor Party.
    In 1878 Sorge and the other Socialists who had
quit this party decided to concentrate their energies
upon strengthening the American labor union movement.
They formed the International Labor Union (ILU), which
advocated the abolition of child and convict labor, the
establishment of special labor bureaus, greater safety
measures at workshops and in the mines, employers'
liability for workingmen's injuries sustained at their
place of work, and shorter working hours, as well as
higher wages. The importance of this new labor union
consisted of the fact that it was the first United
States labor organization which appealed to the large
pool of unskilled laborers in this country. Never
exceeding 8000 members, the ILU went out of existence
in 1887. The demise of the ILU also marked the end of
Sorge's active career as a labor organizer.
    Disillusioned by his failure to set the American
labor movement upon a Marxist basis and beset by severe
bouts of arthritis, Sorge now decided to retire to his
home at Hoboken, New Jersey for the remaining years of
his life. It was here that he was visited during the
summer of 1888 by Friedrich Engels who urged Sorge to
write a history of the American labor movement for Die
Neue Zeit. Not only was Sorge eminently qualified to
write such a history because of his own involvement in
the development of American socialism, but because he
also had for decades gathered a huge collection of
material which included his extensive correspondence
with leading American labor leaders, his voluminous
exchange of letters with Marx and Engels, and the
archives of the First International, which had been left

to his care when that organization was dissolved in 1876.
     There are two major differences between the first
volume of Sorge's Labor Movement in the United States
and the present book. The first volume covered many
occurrences in which Sorge had played a personal role.
In describing the events related in the present volume,
Sorge acted as a mere observer, though hardly an
impartial one. Furthermore, the first book covered the
entire history of American labor from the Colonial Period
until 1890. The current work focuses on only five years:
1892 through 1896. These five years, however, witnessed
a number of momentous developments in the history of the
American labor movement.
     By far the most significant event of those years
was the Pullman Strike of 1894 to which Sorge devoted
three chapters (chs. 7, 8 and 9). It was the first
general strike in American history which affected all
sections of the country. The Pullman strikers, backed
not only by Debs' American Railway Union, but also by
all of American labor, were on the verge of emerging
victoriously from their struggle when the federal government, led by President Grover Cleveland and his Attorney-
General Richard Olney (a former railroad attorney),
waded into the fray on the side of management and, by
the use of troops and court injunctions, crushed the
strike.
     What emerges clearly from Sorge's account is the
fact that the bloody showdown could have been avoided
because the strikers and their leaders were willing to
compromise all along in order to arrive at a solution.
But George Pullman, backed by the powerful General
Managers' Association (consisting of the managers of 24
railroad lines), refused to make even the slightest
concession. The aim of Pullman and the GMA was not only
to defeat the current strike, but also to destroy Debs'
American Railway Union, which had been successful in
uniting many railroad workers who had heretofore been
divided into an array of separate unions (the Brotherhood of Locomotive Engineers, the Brotherhood of Locomotive Firemen, the Brotherhood of Railroad Breakmen,
etc.).
     To a Marxist like Sorge, the Cleveland administra-
tion's actions in regard to the Pullman Strike clearly
showed that it did not really matter whether a Democrat
(like Glover Cleveland) or a Republican (like his
predecessor Benjamin Harrison) was president of the
United States. Both political parties were dominated by
capitalist interests which readily sacrificed the aspirations of the working class. The three branches of the
United States' government were viewed by Sorge not as a
three-fold system of "checks and balances," but rather as
three ways of "checking" the advance of labor. Sorge
devoted an entire chapter (ch. 5) to demonstrating the

servility of the judicial system vis-a-vis the owners of
industry. Not all government officials appear as
villains in Sorge's pages. The democratic governor of
Illinois, John Peter Altgeld, who in 1893 pardoned the
survivors of the Anarchist Trial of 1886, and who in
1894 bitterly opposed Grover Cleveland's dispatch of
federal troops to Chicago, is singled out for special
praise.

The Pullman Strike of 1894 was the most spectacular
strike during these eventful five years, but it was only
one of many. There was also the Buffalo Switchmen's
Strike of 1892 which illustrated the need for unity
among all railroad workers (ch. 1); the armed insurrection of Tennessee coal miners against the coal
companies' use of convict labor (ch. 2); the street
car workers' strikes at Brooklyn (1895), Philadelphia
(1895), and Milwaukee (1896); plus numerous other
strikes brought about, in part, by the misery engendered
by the depression of 1893.

Sorge concludes his book with a description of the
presidential campaign of 1896 which pitted William
Jennings Bryan against William McKinley (ch. 15). It
is clear from Sorge's account that he hoped Bryan would
emerge as the winner. Instead the anti-labor McKinley
won the race, a fitting conclusion to Sorge's book
which records an unending series of defeats for labor's
efforts in the 1890s. Ninety years later, an observer
of the American labor scene might detect much in Sorge's
book that seems familiar. Like the strikes in the
1890s, the major strikes of the 1980s (Air Traffic
Controllers, Hormel Meat, TWA Flight Attendants, etc.)
end monotonously in failure. Labor seems to be as
little united as it was then. The American Federation
of Labor (AFL) under its present leadership seems
as conservative and cautious as it was under Samuel
Gompers, and the indebted farmers suffer as much today
as their ancestors suffered in the 1890s. Finally,
Sorge's ideology holds even less attraction for American
labor today than it did during the last decades of his
life. Plus ca change, plus c'est la même chose!

New Orleans, Louisiana

Summer of 1986

FRIEDRICH A. SORGE'S
Labor Movement
in the United States

1
Buffalo

Early in the morning on August 13th, the switchmen in one of the largest railroad stations in Buffalo went on strike, and on the same morning of August 13th, Tennessee miners, with weapons in their hands, drove convicts from a mine at Tracy City. It appears as a planned simultaneous advance at several points along the lines of battle but in reality it is purely a coincidental concurrence of events during a turbulent period, a concurrence, however, which has sent terror into the hearts of the mighty (i.e., the members of the ruling class who sit at the top of the ladder) as well as the Philistines who have hardly recovered from the fright which the events of Homestead and Idaho gave them. The sedative, the opiate for the timid bourgeois spirits was the National Guard!

The legislature of the State of New York, where Buffalo is located, had issued during its last session (winter of 1892) a Ten Hour Law for railway employees, i.e., for railway servants, switchmen, watchmen, etc. Its own interests dictated it to come forth with this law because of the frequent railroad accidents in this free country (caused for the most part by the exhaustion of the employees) which threaten the lives of the bourgeois passengers as well as the "honorable" members of the legislature. The law was also issued because of the pressure of diverse labor unions. Basing themselves upon this law and possessing a strong organization, the switchmen began to demand a shortening of their work hours and for this purpose entered into negotiations with the railroad officials. These officials, however, either rejected their demands or refused to even listen to them because the law, like all labor protective laws here, had a loop hole through which the railway directors could save themselves and their undiminished profits from the workers.

The influence of the railway corporations upon the legislature of this country is known around the world and is not solely based upon the bourgeois respect for the gigantic capital which the railways possess, but also upon their creatures in the legislative bodies, especially in the "third house" i.e., the agents of the railways in the lobbies of the legislatures. These agents are almost without exception wily lawyers, who are not only interested in pushing through laws on behalf of their employers, but who also try to thwart any decision that is injurious to their employers by rendering it ineffective through the use of harmless-looking ambiguous phraseology. The method that was used in this case consisted of attaching an amendment to the law which stated that overtime (more than 10 hours of work) had to be paid separately. The amendment undermined the Ten Hour Bill or placed it at the mercy of the railway managers.

The shortening of the working hours and the amelioration of the workers' conditions, which the naive minds of the uninitiated might detect in this law, were thus obstructed by most railway managers by the abolition of daily, weekly and monthly wages and their replacement by a reduced hourly wage. The switchmen, who are probably the worst paid workers on the railroads, grumbled, met in their lodges (they are, for the most part, secretly organized), formulated their complaints and demands, submitted them to the railway managers and when they were not listened to, they went out on strike.

Several years ago, the State of New York established a board of mediation and arbitration which on such occasions usually holds an investigation at the scene but exercises no power whatsoever. Before this state board, the switchman, John McMahon, testified that there exists a grievance committee of workers (in this case of switchmen) in every large station, that this committee was established to investigate all complaints and to settle conflicts, that this committee submitted the complaints and demands of the people on June 16th to department superintendent, Bruce, that this man only pointed to the bad financial situation of the railway (Erie), that the committee then traveled to New York in order to speak with the top manager, that they were not able to meet him until a few days later at Buffalo, that their requests were rejected, that the switchmen then unanimously decided to strike, that they had to work for 12 hours with only half an hour for lunch, that they frequently had to work overtime and were not paid for it. Joseph Boss and Matthew Colgan, two switchmen of the Lehigh Valley Railroad, testified that on certain occasions the crew had to work for 36 hours without interruption, while 17, 18, and 20 hours of work without sleep or a lunch break were quite common. The above-

named Joseph Boss revealed on the witness stand that on
June 3rd an announcement was made that starting with May
22nd the hourly wage would be 19, 20 and 22 1/2 cents,
that formerly they had been paid on a monthly basis and
had worked regularly from 12 to 14 hours, that the
announced wages were from 3 to 5 cents an hour less than
previously, that their monthly salary had been short of
5 to 8 dollars which was blamed on an office clerk and
later corrected, that the workers regarded this
procedure as a circumvention of the Ten Hour Law, that
they had to be ready to work at any time and that some
had to work 18 hours a day, that he himself has had to
work from 7 a.m. until 2 p.m., that they were given no
exact time to eat, that they had not a minute to eat or
sleep even when they worked from 12 to 14 hours, that
they were only able to grab a bite to eat for a minute
and only once every 14 days were given an hour lunch
break, that they submitted their complaints to the
general superintendent and after several days had
received a negative response from yet another
superintendent, that the committee went to Philadelphia
in order to meet with the top official Sweigard who
informed them through an office clerk that he would not
receive them and would not listen to them, that they
then submitted their request to the office clerk who
passed it on to the general agent, whereupon the latter
informed them that "Mr. Sweigard positively refuses to
have an interview with these people," that they then
submitted the matter to their lodge and that the members
unanimously (in written form) decided to strike.
Matthew Colgan, the next witness, confirmed the
testimony of the previous witness and testified besides
that he, too, had to work uninterruptedly up to 36 hours
and that he was 24 hours without food.
     George Dutton testified that he, too, had worked
for 36 hours uninterruptedly and that he had often
worked three times a week for 18 and 19 hours without
food. Several others testified similarly, and F. H.
Barmen stated that his work card had been falsified by
supervisor McHoman so that it would show 11 hours when
in reality he had worked 16 or 17 hours. Others
testified that they had been punished for their
participation in the negotiations even though these were
non-union people.
     The grand master (highest official) of the
Switchmen's Union, Sweeney, testified that all of his
efforts in respect to the railway directors had been in
vain--that he had received for the most part only
evasive answers, that he had not ordered a strike which
he had no right to proclaim anyway, and that the people
themselves had voted unanimously to go out on strike.
     How much this strike was justified may be seen from
these testimonies, to which numerous others could be
added and a bitter fight could certainly be expected

after the workers had been treated and injured in such a
despicable manner. Buffalo, however, happens to be one
of the most important railroad junctions of the entire
railway network of the United States and Canada. It is
situated at the extreme northwest of the State of New
York, not far from Canada, at the shore of Lake Erie,
whose outlet, the Niagara, forms the famous Niagara
Falls a few miles from the city. It also constitutes
the terminus as well as the point of departure for the
important trade of the Great Lakes of Superior,
Michigan, Huron and Erie, which are all interconnected
and which form the natural road of communication, the
great water route from the Northwest and the Mid-West of
the country to the East and the Atlantic Ocean. Up to
and beyond Buffalo, the granary of the continent--
Dakota, Minnesota, Wisconsin, Iowa, Illinois, Michigan
and even Canada--sends the greater part of its harvest
and via Buffalo they receive in return the major part of
the industrial products that they need. In Buffalo,
therefore, terminate a large number of the most
important railroads of the United States and Canada and
from Buffalo runs the important Erie Canal to the Hudson
and to the harbor of New York. Tremendous interests are
concentrated at Buffalo and the traffic there is
extremely active, especially at the time of the harvest.
Thus there was enough reason for the capitalist
employers to take this fight very seriously, and the
means that they adopted accordingly do not leave the
slightest doubt that unscrupulousness is a desired and
necessary characteristic of bourgeois administrative
officials and directors.
    The job of a switchman requires no particular skill
but rather a certain degree of strength and common sense
as well as considerable perseverance and the ability to
endure hunger, thirst, and sleeplessness, according to
the reported testimonies. Since both immigrant and
native-born proletarians of this country have made
special studies for the last-named job, and since they
have achieved a recognized skill in it, the supply of
"hands" is always greater than the demand for them, so
that the first task of the striking switchmen was to
keep away the scabs which could hardly be done without
intimidation and threats. This expedient was, indeed,
used successfully, particularly in Buffalo where the
majority of the population sympathized with the strikers
and for a few days it seemed as if the switchmen would
be successful since only one big railroad, the Delaware
and Lackawanna Railroad, remained unmolested because it
had treated its employees relatively well. The other
distressed railroads made the attempt to use the
Delaware and Lackawanna Railroad to take care of their
most urgent orders, but the workers of that railroad
refused to handle such freight with the silent approval
of the railroad's management which was furiously

attacked for this attitude. A New York newspaper,
asked, for example: "What kind of administration does
the Delaware and Lackawanna Railroad have, and on which
kind of morality does it base itself?" The gentlemen
thus confess that there are different sorts of morality.
They are right. Bourgeois institutions use bourgeois
morality and bourgeois principles whose major
commandment is the attainment of the greatest profit in
every conceivable way and certainly at the expense of
the competitor.

The strike began to spread to neighboring towns,
the scabs were either gently or roughly kept away and
the freight began to pile up in gigantic amounts. What
was to be done? To call out the Pinkertons was
prohibited in the state of New York, but there was the
National Guard which had performed such excellent
services in the neighboring state of Pennsylvania. Why
could they not perform similarly in New York? Thus, let
us call the National Guard! There was a catch however!
The man who had to authorize this was the highest
judicial official in the county, the sheriff, and this
man did not favor the calling up of the National Guard
because he believed that the local police would be able
to maintain order. This foolish man had to be brought
to reason, which was brought about by a series of
conflagrations in the stations, which broke out just in
time and destroyed almost nothing except a bunch of
discarded freight cars which had only been a nuisance
for the company. In the meantime, the bourgeois press
saw to it that the Philistines were scared to death and
the sheriff called up the county's National Guard, the
4th Brigade, which used its several hundred men to
occupy the stations. Much to the amusement of the
public, the strikers kept the National Guard busy and
breathless, which hurt the spoiled little brats so much
that they were ready to shoot and were kept from doing
so only with great efforts by the police who, all in
all, behaved rather decently to the strikers. Just what
kind of mood existed vis-a-vis the National Guard is
illustrated by the following small episode: In the
afternoon of August 16th there was a group of strikers
near a station when a detachment of the National Guard
marched by. "Why do you not take off your hat before
the soldiers, Tom?" one of the strikers sneeringly asked
his neighbor. "What, take my hat off before these
little dolls?" answered the other. "If I had a good
club, I would chase the whole bunch of them back to the
arsenal!"

The levy of the local guard troop did not harm the
strike much, and the pressed railroad companies were not
able to move the enormously growing pile of freight.
The big New York Central Railroad did not want to try to
move anything until it had the entire forces of the
state at its disposal. The employees of the railroads,

the engineers, firemen, brakemen, etc., aided the
switchmen with a peculiarly passive method: they
absolutely refused to touch anything that did not
pertain to their special jobs. A reporter from Buffalo
writes: "The same mood also exists among the police for
the most part." Yesterday (August 17th) a completely
equipped and manned freight train stood at Seneca Street
from 11 a.m. until 4 p.m. because there was nobody to
move a switch which was located only a few feet from the
train. The locomotive was under full steam, the
engineer and the firemen manned their posts, but the
train might as well have been lying at the bottom of a
near ditch because it was absolutely motionless. A
reporter asked a policeman who was standing near the
switch what was the matter. "There is nobody to move
the switch." was the answer. "Well, why do you not it
yourself?" asked the reporter. "I am not being paid for
this. I am not going to touch the switch!" replied the
policeman. The train personnel answered in a similar
fashion.

Such a situation did not, of course, please the
railroad companies, least of all the directors of the
New York Central Railroad (Vanderbilt's line). If
Pennsylvania had called up its entire National Guard in
order to tame Homestead, New York could not hold back as
far as Buffalo was concerned. Therefore, the New York
Central Railroad did not move any freight as vice-
president Webb (notorious since 1890) put it: "Until
one guarantees us better protection, more soldiers are
needed to give our people absolute security. We still
have not given up our plan to obtain more soldiers. We
will ask the mayor who has as much right to call for
these soldiers as the sheriff." But the mayor was in no
mood to assume this responsibility and now there was a
critical situation. The burning of old, discarded
freight cars did not work anymore, because the opinion
had spread among the public that the railroad companies
had done it for their own benefit. A real genuine
insurrection just did not come about in spite of the
clumsy acts and the provocations on the part of the
immature guardsmen. The police maintained a certain
neutrality and the sheriff did not do more than he
absolutely had to. Everything was now done to change
the sheriff's mind. A reporter for a bourgeois
newspaper writes: "It was a hard job. The railroad men
had to convince the sheriff that it was really necessary
to call on the governor for the troops, because the
sheriff viewed the situation as less dangerous and he
did not want to burden the county with the unnecessary
daily expenditure of $25,000." The railroad officials
and directors moved heaven and earth to change the man's
mind. They asked for the help of all members of the
upper bourgeoisie, the lawyers and the politicians.
They besieged the mayor of the city and called one

meeting after another of the prominent people of the
town in their elegant clubs where they could be just
amongst each other. The sheriff, due to the approaching
general elections, was reluctant to take extreme
measures and he was not independent enough to ignore the
constant importunities and molestations of this gang of
big crooks and to slam the door in their faces.
Instead, he followed their invitations to attend their
meetings where he argued with them. At the penultimate
gathering he told them: "Today I marched along the
entire line of the strikers and I did not observe a
single act of violence . . . ." The above-mentioned
Webb screamed at the sheriff: "Do you mean to tell me
that it is not your obligation to protect the railroads
during the exercise of their business activities if they
are prevented from doing so by rebellious persons?"
"That is certainly my duty," answered the sheriff, "but
I am not of the opinion that an emergency situation
exists, and I have been told by outstanding citizens
that it is up till now unnecessary to call for more
troops." An ex-judge by the name of Brundage, a worthy
crony of the railroad magnates asked: "Are you
insisting upon not asking the governor for more National
Guard troops?" "That is my point of view," replied the
sheriff, "unless the situation gets worse." "Then we
will be damned if we will talk to you any longer!"
screamed McMillan, a state senator from New York, and
the whole gang rushed out of the meeting place in order
to consult in a private office how they could get to the
sheriff. A little bit later they returned, had another
hot battle of words with the sheriff and finally
obtained his assurance that he would demand more troops.
The man, who had become weary and exhausted by this
nocturnal debate, telegraphed the governor during this
same night in the early morning hours, and on the
evening of the same day (August 18th) the reinforcements
were already arriving. Within 48 hours, almost the
entire National Guard of the state, about 8,000 men,
followed, to be employed against 800 strikers. The
presidents, vice-presidents, superintendents, agents,
etc., of the railroads happily rubbed their hands and
the scabs went to work.
     The National Guard was not received in a
particularly friendly manner, and it is understandable
that the strikers developed a deep animosity towards
them and did not hesitate to express it. A reporter
writes: "Nothing demonstrates the spirit of anarchy (!)
better than the treatment of the soldiers on the part of
the strikers and their followers. They (the National
Guardsmen) are being cursed, stoned and insulted in
every possible way. Today (August 21st), Captain Thyng
of the 43rd Company got tired of the insults on the part
of a crowd of supporters of the strikers who, from a
distance were throwing small pieces of coal at the

soldiers, and ran out in front of them, screaming:
"Stop this immediately, or we will give you a piece of
lead for every piece of coal!" The coal throwing
stopped, but one person in the crowd yelled to the
soldiers: "We cannot fight with coal against lead, but
we would like to have about 20 minutes with you on equal
terms (with similar weapons) to give you a lesson for
coming here and interfering in our business!"

     This mood against the National Guard was by no
means confined to the strikers but was shared by the
majority of the population who did not like the railroad
management and acted accordingly whenever the
circumstances permitted. A report from New York states
as follows: "The National Guardsmen received a very
cool reception at Hoverly (a station along the Erie
Railroad) where the entire population seems to be intent
on making their lives as uncomfortable as possible. The
mayor of the town, Charles Shipman, who was being
pressured by the entire population, ordered Captain
Olmsted to remove immediately his men and guns from the
streets of the town and to station them outside the town
limits (this order was carried out) . . . During the
evening of the same day, the citizens of the town held a
mass meeting where they expressed their indignation over
the call-up of the National Guard and took steps towards
their removal.

     Nevertheless, the National Guard was there and the
strikers could not use their primary weapon which was to
work upon the scabs by persuasion, intimidation or
threats. There remained for them only one expedient: an
appeal to the closest and nearest unions and workers'
organizations, the brakemen, firemen, engineers and
conductors that all possessed strong organizations and
well-filled coffers. A few years ago, they had formed a
sort of syndicate of mutual assistance under certain
circumstances but only for a limited time, and that had
expired last winter. They had, however, always
maintained certain relations by a more or less regular
exchange of information and it seemed only natural that
an appeal for help should be directed towards these
organizations. If these organizations could be
persuaded to ally themselves with the switchmen and to
make the latter's cause their own, then, the switchmen
could well count on a victory because the railway
directors would hardly dare to take on their entire
personnel. The often voiced spirit or brotherliness and
community of interests had to be put to the test, and
Grand Master Sweeney called together by telegraph the
other grand masters[2] for consultations. The heads of
the conductors, firemen, and brakemen all appeared while
the chief of the engineers, Mr. Arthur, was conspicuous
by his absence--as everybody expected since the
exclusivity and conservatism of this gentleman were only
too well known. His absence could only be interpreted

to mean that the engineers did not want to become
involved, and that sealed the fate of the switchmen
since no other organization wanted to join the battle
without the simultaneous and uniform participation of
all of the others. The conference of the grand masters
took place on August 24th and immediately thereafter
Grand Master Sweeney declared the strike of the
switchmen as ended. Already on August 26th the National
Guardsmen, who did not leave behind a very good
reputation, began their return journey.

The test of the fraternal spirit of the
consciousness of brotherhood among such closely related
branches of work as the above-mentioned ones has failed
this time, but the feeling of solidarity is present,
even if it is latent at the moment, and it will sooner
or later come to the fore in order to weld the railway
workers together in spite of Mr. Arthur and his sad
associates. The most effective mainspring of this
solidarity is the unceasing, ongoing, leveling of wage
labor which will hardly stop in front of the
organization of engineers. The grumbling against the
latter has become ever more pronounced among all the
strata of the working class, but particularly among the
other branches of the railroad employees, and it is an
open secret that the firemen are very unhappy with the
attitude of the engineers. A short while ago, the
secretary and treasurer of the firemen's union resigned
because of that and assumed instead the editorship of
its special paper with the following words: "The
federation of all railroad employees has been the task
of my life. To unite all of them in one body is my
goal. But I do not believe that it will be possible to
do along the present lines. Now the people are
organized in classes with distinct points of departure.
Class stratification favors class prejudices and class
egotism and instead of approaching one another, the
tendency is present to keep one another apart. Given
the present differences in the organizations and among
the big officials, a federation is practically
impossible. My life's greatest goal has been the
unification of all railroad employees and the extinction
of the labor aristocracy (which unfortunately exists)
and the organization of all workers upon an equal basis.
All my efforts will be pointed in this direction."

In order to understand this quotation, one has to
know the phraseology of the American labor leaders and
editors which is filled with veiled modes of expressions
and vagueness that are caused by a certain lack of
courage. When he speaks of "classes," this otherwise
estimable man means the members of the different
branches of the railway service, the skilled and
unskilled workers, those with higher and lower salaries;
in other words--the engineers and firemen, the
conductors and brakemen. The "differences in the

organization" relate to the fact that the engineers
require from the job candidates a certificate of skill
(a sort of facultas docendi). The conductors, on the
other hand, require proof that the candidate has a
certain amount of money because they have to give
security. The "difference among the big officials"
refers to the greater esteem which the officers of the
just mentioned organizations claim for their particular
outfits which they proudly assert towards the
economically less well-off categories.
     The official organ of the "United Mine Workers of
America" accompanied the above-cited comments with the
following words:

> Probably never before has the resignation of a
> labor union official been so grievously regretted
> and deplored as that of the secretary and
> treasurer of the united firemen. . . . that Mr.
> Debs (that is the name of the man) has resigned
> from his position in order to become the editor of
> the organ of the firemen and to pursue his goals
> with greater freedom; let us surmise that he had
> been fettered to a certain degree in his official
> capacity. We cannot help but express our
> undisguised pleasure over the fact that such an
> honorable and deep-thinking man as Debs decided to
> work on the liquidation of the labor aristocracy.
> . . . His words, 'that given the present
> differences between the big officials,' easily
> reveal that one or more individuals in high
> offices of the railway brotherhoods have used
> their influence in order to bend others to their
> will. Some of our papers view the natural death
> of the president (who acts half Caesar, half
> Diogenes, and is regarded as the chief obstacle to
> Mr. Debs' plan) as the best solution to the
> question which is of great interest to the
> engineers. It seems to us that it is quite a nice
> and pretty position for a man to be in who tells
> the assembled delegates of a certain union that
> they are more intelligent and more educated and in
> every way more favored than the other labor
> branches with which they have indeed nothing in
> common. That is the talk of a man who has almost
> succeeded in creating a labor aristocracy, but in
> contrast stand the heartwarming words of Debs who
> is as highly respected by his constituents as a
> human being can possibly be. And since the man
> who directs the fate of the engineers with all of
> his cynical slyness has not been able to produce a
> labor aristocracy because its elements resist
> crystallization, it is quite certain that Mr.
> Debs' plan will certainly triumph. The strike of
> the switchmen at Buffalo as well as many other

examples prove that in spite of temporary
compromise and favoritism toward the privileged
branch of labor, the time will come when this
privileged caste will, for their own protection,
ally themselves with those who, were they in such
a mood during the hour of need, could immediately
destroy all the assured ideas about a labor
aristocracy."

The language is already much clearer and the leading
thoughts unequivocal.Let us hope that actions will follow
and that there will soon be solid connections between all
the railway employees. Then even the defeat of the
switchmen will have rendered considerable services to the
labor movement of the country.

2
Tennessee

As has been previously reported, on that same day of August 13th, 1892, the miners of Tennessee, with weapons in their hands, drove the convicts from the mines at Tracy City, and following this deed, a series of similar events occurred in the mines of Tennessee. A short description of these events and their outcome will be preceded by a substantial account of the system of convict labor, particularly as it exists in the former slave states, to which Tennessee belongs, and its connection with the events of 1891.

With the increase of the population grows the number of the inmates of jails, penitentiaries or other penal institutions, and with the progress of [1] "civilization" mounts the number of convicts who have to be kept busy and made to perform useful work. The bourgeois society as well as the bourgeois economy, however, understand usefulness as profit and being useful as being profitable or gainful--not for those that do the work but rather for those righteous, well-behaved citizens who are not yet in jail, who cause this work to be carried out while they do not move so much as a finger. It is well-known how these (work) free citizens exploit the (property) free workers by allowing surplus value to be created, i.e., more is produced than is necessary for the maintenance and reproduction of the work force. It is from this surplus value that they derive their profits, which must be very significant given the colossal wealth and incomes of the prominent citizens of the industrially developed countries. If "free" work already garners such gains for the non-workers, how much more, calculate these honorable citizens, must penal labor yield, whose cost of maintenance and reproduction is, or should be, far less, especially since the state always pays part of the cost which is not charged to any account. Just as "civilization" fills the jails, so it must also fill the purses of the free and honest citizens of this highly civilized country, who make every effort, sometimes even with philanthropic phraseology, to put the work of the convicts to useful purposes: namely for the production of cheap goods.

This intramural production of cheap goods in the penitentiary, however, became quite competitive with the extramural production of goods. It pushed down the prices of the respective goods and cut the wages of the workers outside the prison walls. It created, therefore, in countries which have strong labor movements, a strong opposition against unfair competition of prison work. The abolition of this competition² has been a constant demand at workers' congresses² for 30 years and frequently achieved practical recognition in industrial states, e.g., in New York, Massachusetts, New Jersey, etc. Since the mining of coal has spread to the southern states of this country, the use of convicts in the coal mines of several former slave states has become very popular. Since the end of the 1870's, i.e., since the strengthening of the coal miners' organizations, all workers' conventions have issued resolutions against the use of convict labor in the mines but without any real success in the characteristic states (Tennessee, Kentucky, Missouri, Georgia, Alabama, etc.). The greater the demand for coal grew in the "New South", the more the coal mining regions there were expanding, the more profitable became the employment of convicts in the mines and all the more threatening also became the attitude of the coal miners who were fighting for their existence against this competition.

The most threatened coal miners, those of Tennessee, were almost all native Americans who had originally settled that area and maintained their fine traditions. For more than 100 years, the mountains and valleys of present day East Tennessee had been settled by a strong and independent group of people that not only distinguished themselves during the War of Independence by their bravery, but later on, too, defended their rights and liberties, often with weapons in their hands. During the Civil War (1861-1865), East Tennessee had remained loyal to the Union, even though the legislature of the state had come out for the secession, and sent its sons to the Northern armies. From this healthy, unspoilt breed of people, the miners were recruited, and it happened to be these people who were bereft of their livelihood by the occupation of the mines and, in many cases, required to work together with the convicts. When all of their protests against these measures remained fruitless, they were already driven to open rebellion in 1891.

The subsequent description of the causes and the
course of this rebellion of 1891 consists of verbatim
excerpts from official documents, namely the special
report of the commissioner of labor and inspector of
mines to his excellency the governor etc., etc. and from
the message of Governor John P. Buchanan to the 47th
General Assembly, Special Session of August 31st, 1891.
The legislature had issued a law on March 26th,
1887, which gave every mine the right to elect from its
midst, a check weighman and a check measurer. When the
commissioner of labor and inspector of mines wanted to
inspect the Tennessee mine at Briceville on April 16th,
1891, he was told at the entrance that the company had
suspended work at the mine until the workers had signed
a contract stating that they would work without a check
weighman. The workers complained furthermore (and were
able to prove) that in the company stores in which they
often had to shop because there was only one pay day a
month, they were charged 20 to 30% more than in other
stores (truck system). They were also harassed if they
were not regular clients in the company stores in spite
of a law dated the same as the one just mentioned which
prohibits all pressure and intimidation of workers and
holds out punishment in case of
violation of this law. On June 12th, the president of
the mining company, Jenkins, told the miners that the
company would employ convicts if the miners would not
sign the above-mentioned contract. With few exceptions,
the workers refused to sign. Some did, went to work and
were called "blacklegs", but there were not enough of
them to keep the mine running, and on Sunday morning,
July 5th, a whole wagonload of 40 convicts came and were
told immediately to fix up dwellings which heretofore
had been inhabited by miners so that a further shipment
of convicts, which was expected on July 15th, could be
put up.
The inhabitants of the entire valley, men of the
most diverse trades and professions, now became alarmed
and held meetings to discuss the situation and to come
to a decision as to the removal of the convicts from the
valley, which had become a matter of general public
interest for all of the valley's inhabitants in addition
to the miners. Until the arrival of the convicts, the
cause of the miners was represented in a peaceful and
orderly manner by the Knights of Labor, but the miners
could no longer be so easily led after their cause had
become a matter of common interest. The "blacklegs"
were now the most violent accusers of the company and
demanded most loudly the removal of the convicts, an
effort in which they were supported by the store owners
and real estate proprietors. On July 14th, a meeting of
miners and citizens of the valley was held and it was
decided to approach the enclosure of the mine and demand
the removal of the 40 convicts from the valley.

Equipped with Winchester rifles, old muskets, hunting
rifles and revolvers, the crowd that numbered 300 men
moved through the valley to the enclosure, which they
reached between 12 and 1 p.m. They demanded the
surrender of the convicts which was agreed to without a
fight. The convicts were led to Coal Creek, put into
empty railroad wagons and put into the county jail at
Knoxville.

The superintendent of the jail and the county
sheriff telegraphed to the governor for military
assistance. The Citizens' Committee of the People's
Assembly also telegraphed and asked for protection from
the importation of convicts in order to prevent
bloodshed--which would be inevitable if one would
persist in cutting off the livelihood of the inhabitants
and miners. At noon on July 16th, the governor,
accompanied by the three National Guard companies,
brought the convicts back to Briceville and on that same
afternoon spoke to an assembly of miners and inhabitants
of the valley. He told them it was his duty to see to
it that the laws of the state were carried out, that the
assembled people should not take the law into their own
hands, that the popularly-elected legislature had made
the laws whose justice or equity was not up to him to
judge, that he had done much to help them (the workers),
that injustice could not be overcome by rebellions
actions but by the silent ballot box which would
determine the election of men who would give them just
laws, that their complaints could not be resolved by
violence, that if they were to persist in their behavior
they would get into even greater trouble, etc.

Eugene Merrill, the chairman of the assembly, spoke
after the governor and said among other things: "I am
not criticizing the governor because of the stand that
he has taken, because he is obligated to act that way.
But he does not know the number and the extent of our
complaints or he does not pay enough attention to them.
It is all very nice to preach obedience to the law. The
proprietors and exploiters of the mines can violate the
laws without facing punishment and all that the miners
can do against them is to put up with the injustice that
is placed upon them. The governor says that the law is
designed to fight injustice. Why then is the law not
used when the exploiters commit injustice?" The speaker
then enumerated all the injustices and violations of the
law which employers commit: the truck system, the
cheating in the company stores, the issuing of coupons
instead of money, the rejection of the controllers, the
intimidations and other measures. He concluded: "Is
there no protection? Will the governor and the
officials do anything whatsoever for us while they are
dispatching the National Guard to assist Mr. Morrow (the
overseer of the mine at Briceville): Will they as
readily send the National Guard to protect us from

injustice if the company decides to shut the mine in
order to circumvent the law concerning the controllers?
The miners do not want to violate the law, but they want
to protect themselves as well as their wives and
children and they will do so!"

During the following night, a large gathering was
held which appointed an executive committee of 12 men.
On the 18th yet another big meeting was held during
which certain compromise proposals of labor commissioner
Ford were rejected and an ultimatum was made: "No
compromise! The convicts must go!" During the
following night the battle plans were made which were
based upon obtaining the sympathies of the National
Guardsmen: "The miners will not fire upon the National
Guard and we are quite certain that the National Guard
will not fire upon us. They come from the same
background as we do and must, therefore, have sympathy
for us." The Guardsmen were treated with the greatest
kindness, and that seemed to work. On Monday morning,
July 20th, 1891, the railroads were transporting from
everywhere in Tennessee (also from Kentucky)
reinforcements for the miners who, about 1500 strong,
marched to the mine at Briceville and demanded the
removal of the convicts to which Colonel Sevier, who
commanded 107 men, after a brief hesitation, agreed.
From there the miners moved to Coal Creek and succeeded
there, too, to have the convicts removed from the mine
of the Knoxville Iron Company. All these activities
were carried out without the least damage to private or
state property, and on July 21st it was decided to call
a special session of the legislature to abolish the
system of renting out convicts, etc. On July 22nd the
miners' committees and the citizens who sympathized with
them, held a conference with the governor in Knoxville
during which the following proposals were submitted:

1) The restoration of the status quo ante and
   an amnesty for what has occurred.
2) Annulment of the lease contract with the
   Tennessee Coal, Iron and Railway Company.
3) Immediate convocation of the legislature
   in order to abolish the convict rental
   system.
4) Protection of private state property in
   the hands of the miners.
5) Removal of the convicts from Coal Creek
   and Olive Springs as soon as the rental
   system has been abolished.
6) The miners provide for and protect the
   guards of the convicts and the National
   Guard will be sent home.

The following appendix was added: "It is unnecessary on our part to point out the seriousness of the situation. We are neither nihilists nor adherents of the Commune. We fight for the right to earn our bread through honest work, and we are fundamental foes of that system of labor which is used to humiliate us. We appeal to all those who possess humane feelings for both us and our families."

The governor declared that it was his task to restore law and order, that it was indeed true that he had decided to convoke the legislature for a special session which would consider the convict question, the contract system, etc., but that he could make no assurances as to what kind of decisions would be made.

After further meetings, the following new demands were submitted to the governor on July 23rd: 1) Restoration of the status quo; 2) Removal of the National Guard; 3) The declaration of a 60-day truce; 4) Convocation of the legislature and the recommendation that it would revoke the convict rental system; 5) After this revocation, the removal of all convicts from Coal Creek, Briceville and Oliver Springs.

The governor, who had gathered 500 National Guardsmen at Knoxville, did not accept these demands and implored the miners to submit in hope that their complaints would be resolved in a legal manner. The miners and inhabitants of the valley became unnerved and, after long and intense debates, submitted to the governor on July 24th the following last resolutions:

1) The status quo will be restored and the guards and convicts will not be bothered upon their return.
2) With our full confidence in the governor and in the expectation that the legislature, convoked in extraordinary session, will free us from the burdens weighing upon us, we will try to behave as law-abiding citizens in order to preserve thereby the sympathy and the trust of the public for the future, just as we have enjoyed in the past.
3) We herewith express our gratitude to Governor Buchanan for his friendly considerateness in keeping the National Guard in the city (Knoxville), thus preventing conflict and possible bloodshed.
4) We thank our friends and neighbors in the valley for their advice and assistance.

These resolutions were accepted by the governor and on July 25th the militia was sent home and the convicts back into the mines of Coal Creek and Briceville.

So much for the report of the Commissioner of Labor for Tennessee about the unrest during July of 1891. Attached to that report are several reports and protocols of the Board of Supervisors of the State Prisons and a resolution of the latter that declared the above-mentioned mine at Briceville as unfit for work and ordered the prison warden to remove the convicts from there. No less that 10 legal violations are adduced as justifications for this resolution which was fought by the mine owners in court but without success. Information is also given about the lease of convict labor according to which lessees have to pay an annual sum of $100,000 for convict labor. Furthermore, it is reported that three-fourths of all convicts were brought into the mines as strike breakers where they constituted a serious competition to the miners and seriously pushed down the latter.

The governor called together a special session of the legislature on August 31st to decide upon 12 points of which only the following are worth mentioning:

1) Sufficient militia or military power (or both) to be created in order to enable the governor to preserve the law.
2) In the public interest, laws dealing with the work, leasing or guarding of convicts, the removal, new construction or augmentation of state prisons, measures to prevent contracts and the competition between convicts and free laborers, are to be revoked, changed or issued.
3) Laws are to be issued to change and improve the criminal code of the state; furthermore, laws are to be decreed against the distribution of coupons instead of money and against any interference in the affairs of the state convicts.

The subsequent additional excerpt from the report is of interest: First of all, a revision of the criminal code is necessary because the code was issued before the present state of society, when the masters still ruled over their own plantations and applied physical punishment for minor offenses. Of the 1500 inmates of the state prisons, 1008 are black and the major part of them have been convicted for minor offenses. Minor and major crimes should be kept separate in such a way that those convicted of minor crimes are kept in the county jail and only serious criminals are sent to the state prisons. Every county could then employ its prisoners in construction of streets or bridges and in agriculture. These prisoners could be more easily guarded and made into better people

if they were not thrown together with the hardened
criminals, and the state penitentiary would lose 50% of
its inmates. Indeed, the report continues, the state
penitentiary should only contain those people whose
freedom would be dangerous for society . . . The aim of
penal legislation ought to be the protection of society,
the prevention of crime and the betterment of the
criminal, not revenge and punishment.
. . . The governor reports that in the United States
four different forms of convict labor are used: 1)
Convicts employed solely by the state. This is
evidently the best method, but it is used only in
Arizona and California. 2) The contract system by which
the convict's work is given to the highest bidder--a
method used in most states. 3) The piece work system,
whereby a contractor pays the state a certain price for
the delivered product. 4) The rent and lease system,
whereby the entire work of a convict is rented for a
year (under certain conditions) for a certain sum. This
method is in use in most of the former slave states as
well as in Nebraska, Washington and New Mexico. It is
the method which guarantees the state the greatest
income and frees it of all business risks or costs. The
governor recommends a system of work based upon a
monthly bill if the penal code should be altered, but if
the legislature "in its wisdom" should keep the old
system, then one should try to persuade the lessees to
make certain changes so that the worst aspects may be
ameliorated somewhat. At the end of his report he
points to the report of the labor commissioner about the
unrest at Briceville and Coal Creek.
    The report of the labor commissioner is
distinguished by its objectivity, that of the governor
by its indecisiveness. The legislature "in its wisdom"
did not do anything to resolve the complaints of the
miners. They also left the lease contract in tact since
the company that was the lessee, the Tennessee Coal,
Iron and Railway Company, firmly struck to its
agreement.
    It is understandable that the miners were in an
irritable mood after their justified complaints were
treated with such disdain. If until then they had
discussed and decided everything in frank and open
meetings, they now met secretly in order to contemplate
what they should do next. After all the preparations
had been made, more than 2000 inhabitants of the valley
attacked the mine and the convict barracks of Briceville
on the evening of October 30th, overpowered the guards,
freed the convicts and burned down the barracks and the
enclosures. In order that the convicts would not be
brought back as they had been before, they were given
ordinary bourgeois clothes and told to get lost,
preferably across the state's borders. So that they
would not be taken by surprise, they cut telegraph wires

in all directions. The bourgeois press driveled
sensationally about a considerable number of dead and
wounded, but without any cause, because the guards had
not had any time to attempt any resistance. On November
2nd at 1 a.m. about 200 men on horseback descended the
mountains towards Oliver Springs, liberated the local
convicts just as had been done at Briceville, and burned
down the barracks without injuring anyone. Thus about
500 convicts were set free and most of them fled to
Kentucky. The governor set a reward for their recapture
and for the seizure of the ringleaders of the miners,
but he did not want to call up the National Guard once
more. The mine owners now tried to employ blacks who
were, however, chased away. Warrants were issued for
the arrest of about ten miners, but only two could be
found and convicted, whereupon all miners stopped their
work. Coal Creek in the end received a regular military
occupation by National Guard troops--and all of this
happened in the year 1891 as a prelude to the battles
and the unrest of August 1892. Here follows a brief
description of the latter.

     The first thrust this time occurred in the more
southerly situated district, in Tracy City, where a
large number of free workers had to work next to about
300 convicts in the coal mines. The free workers had
their time³ and wages cut and their complaints about
this had been ignored. They decided to take matters
into their own hands. Well armed and well prepared,
they ambushed the mines on the morning of August 13th,
led the convicts away, and burnt down the barracks. Two
days later iron mines at Inman were captured. On August
17th the coal mines at Oliver Springs and on August 18th
those of Coal Creek were taken, the latter only after a
hard fight. The tactic of establishing a good
relationship with the National Guard, which had been
employed during the past year, had been generally used
again, but at Coal Creek there had been frequent
vexations during the past eight months between the
population and the National Guard, which had been
stationed there permanently since last winter. A unit
of approximately 100 men had constructed there a small
armed camp near the mine. The troops were led by a
brave man who turned back every attack upon the camp and
rejected every demand to surrender even after he had
been taken prisoner by the assailants. This caused such
a delay that the governor and the authorities were able
to send reinforcements in the form of loyal National
Guard troops from the cities and the southwestern
counties. On August 20th, Coal Creek was once again
seized from the miners.

     This August week in Tennessee did not lack its
serious and funny episodes. It is true that the workers
had used their weapons but, at the same time, they had
relied too much upon their rights and, as always, they

were cheated. They were still not looking far enough beyond the borders of their county or valley. Thus it happened that a delegation of Coal Creek miners were personally pleading with the governor to withdraw the National Guard troops that had been stationed there since the winter, while at the same time the news of the sudden attack at Tracy City arrived. As a result, the delegation beat a hasty retreat and now began the battles at Coal Creek during which the miners even used a small mountain cannon. A number of National Guardsmen and miners were killed. Along with entire trains, various National Guard companies were captured, disarmed and sent home. The naive little people, who did not want to be nihilists or adherents of the Commune, had cut all telegraph wires and undermined the railroad tracks at various spots. Governor Buchanan became very sick and weak after he had called up the National Guard. The National Guard officers accused each other, coram publico, of cowardice and inability.

After Coal Creek fell, i.e., after it had been reoccupied by the National Guard, the latter showed its claws. The miners still held the commander of the previous occupying unit and when they did not immediately hand him over, the commander of the new National Guard occupation force arrested all citizens of the town who, almost without exception, had sympathized with the miners. An intense search was made for the leaders of the movement who were threatened with summary execution if they did not betray their comrades. The representative for Anderson County (where Coal Creek is situated) in the legislature was threatened with arrest, and the commissioner of labor was actually arrested because of sympathies for the miners. By August 24th about 500 people had been arrested. They were locked up in churches and schools and, in the beginning, were given only one meal a day consisting of water and corn bread. They were dragged in front of courts and accused of murder, rebellion, etc.--just like their colleagues in Idaho. The company which held the convict lease contract in their hands quarreled with the authorities for a little while about the further guarding and employment of the convicts, and both of them pretended that they would dissolve the contract; but after a few days, the convicts were brought back to their former places. The politicians now attempted to exploit the whole business to their own advantage. They were led in this effort by Governor Buchanan himself, who joined the 'third party'--the so-called People's Party--in order to stay in office.

The miners have fought in vain. They took one position after another, only to be driven out of them once more and to be subjugated because they practiced parish-pump politics, and they did not advance simultaneously and united. Will they have learned from

this? If they would only get together and build up a
united organization with which they could dictate their
conditions for peace. This was proven by the fact that
this year, as well as last year, a significant number of
Kentucky miners came to their aid voluntarily. It was
also shown by the anxiety that predominated in the
bourgeois circles of the neighboring states.

One lesson, however, has been learned by many
workers of this country from the repeated battles: they
now mistrust the bourgeois National Guard which, much to
the glee of the employers, represented a satisfactory
and cheap substitute for the Pinkertons. The bitterness
which exists among the workers against the Pinkertons is
now beginning to be transferred to the National Guard
which, besides, is showered with grim ridicule. During
the last few months a significant number of unions have
come out with resolutions which oppose the entry of
workers into the National Guard and declare that service
in the National Guard is incompatible with the
obligations towards labor organizations. Very important
in this connection also is the exclusion of the National
Guard companies from the observances of Labor Day in the
various cities of the country; an exclusion which
several unions made as a condition for their own
participation at this celebration. It is a beginning to
free the workers of this bourgeois rubbish.

Much more important would be a closing of the ranks
of the organized laborers who are still meandering in so
many individual organizations and unions. Here and
there, they co-exist peacefully, but unfortunately often
enough, they march against each other instead of facing
unitedly the common foe. During the current year, all
the great unions have been involved in battle and been
hurt: the A.F.L. at Homestead, the Knights of Labor and
the miners in Idaho and Tennessee, and the railroad
workers in Buffalo. Every one of these great
organizations has been beaten because it marched and
fought separately; whereas, every single fight this year
probably would have been successful if everybody had
fought with united strength. No power in this country
would have dared to resist a million workers who were
united defensively and offensively. Undoubtedly the
recognition of this evil is spreading and, as soon as it
pervades the masses, it will lead to a concentration of
forces. If both of the great unions, the A.F.L. and the
Knights of Labor, are equal to their task, their annual
convention this fall will have to undertake important
steps. If it should come to a reasonable rapprochement
between them, then the related battles will not have
been in vain, the blood will not have been shed for no
purpose, and then, even out of defeat, a blessing will
develop for the workers.

The United States find themselves at the time of
this writing in a presidential campaign which is this

time an especially lukewarm affair because the
politicians in the East have a secret fear of the
workers, and the politicians in the West are afraid of
the small farmers. At the nominating conventions of the
Republican and Democratic parties held in Minneapolis
and Chicago at the beginning of the summer, a few pro-
labor phrases were incorporated into the party
platforms, but the nominating speeches of the two
respective candidates, which followed two to three
months later, do not mention the big fights of this year
with a single word. The representatives and leaders of
the bourgeois republic have no need to do so.

Chapter II: Endnotes

[1]The savages and barbarians maintain no penitentiaries.

[2]The demand was also made in England, Germany, and other countries.

[3]This sounds strange and must be explained as follows: the miners there, as in most other coal mines, were paid according to the quantity of coal that they produced. For every ton or "bushel" of coal, they received a certain amount of money. Thus they had to produce a considerable amount of coal in order to earn sufficient wages. The owners of the above-mentioned mine made the convicts work as long as possible, but allowed the free miners to work only for a brief period of time so that the latter did not make enough money to live on and, therefore, complained about short working hours.

3
April 1893

It has previously been pointed out in reports from the United States that the standard bearers of the bourgeois parties of this country did not mention at all in their acceptance speeches (on the occasion of their nomination) the significant events of the year concerning the labor movement and that the representatives of the bourgeoisie simply do not consider this as necessary. The bourgeois republic, which in the United States (according to Karl Marx) represents "the conservative form of life of bourgeois society," does not recognize any class differences and even denies them or imposes silence on them until the class struggle explodes. When it first tries to stir, it either tries to suppress it brutally or it tries to render it harmless by palliatives or phrasemongering. This past year is full of examples of this process.

Even if the bourgeoisie and the Philistines try to defend themselves in this manner against the labor movement or if they try to ignore it, they still know very well that the workers constitute a great political force as voters and as a special interest group. In order that the workers may not be conscious of their class situation and their political clout, the bourgeoisie tries to deceive them by telling them how well off they are under the rule of this or that bourgeois party. The press, the preachers and the officials compete with each other in this distortion and falsification of facts and reports.

It is well known what the European "statesmen" achieved when it comes to the embellishment of facts, but their accomplishments pale before those of the American census officials, statisticians and presidents. Gladstone, Morley, Bismarck, Leon Say, Plener and their accomplices are amateurs in comparison to our Porter

(Superintendent of the Census), Peck (labor statistician) and Harrison (President of the United States).

The portentous events of Homestead, Coeur D'Alene, Buffalo, Tennessee, etc., had to be obliterated and the raging waters calmed by official euphemisms and oratory. There was imminent danger and, lo and behold, the census bureau, so well known for its dilatoriness, pulled itself together and published and sent out, right in the middle of the election campaign, a census bulletin about the statistics of manufacture of a number of the most important cities of the country, wherein the enormous growth of industry and wages was proven (or the attempt was made to prove it). The increase in wages ("a decided relative increase in the amount paid in wages") which, according to local variables, was supposed to fluctuate between 20 to 60% was especially stressed.

The census man, Porter, was followed by the labor statistician of the State of New York, Peck, who published during September of last year a sort of summary of his annual report for the year 1891, a report which was not to be submitted to the legislature until January 1893. In this summary, Peck comes to the following conclusions: "1) . . . 2) In the aggregate and as a rule, with small exceptions, the capital invested in industry has grown to a greater degree than the 'hands' that are employed therein. 3) On the other hand, the total sum of the paid wages has grown to a greater degree than the number of 'hands' and the average wages in 1890 were higher than in 1880. . . . In the City of New York, the annual average wage in 1890 amounted to $653 in comparison to $427 during 1880, an increase of 52.93%. 4) The persons employed in manufacture grew faster than the population. . . . 5) The total value of the products of the factories has not grown in comparison to the growth rate of the invested capital as well as the percentage of the employed 'hands,' even though, as far as we know, the quantity of the products must have grown to a higher degree than the amount of the invested capital and the number of employed workers."

These statistics understandably created a sensation. The Republicans were cheering and the Democrats were cursing and attempting to refute the above mentioned reports' but there was hardly enough time to do so. Then, too, the census man had protected himself to some degree against attempts at refutation by the following comment that preceded his actual report: "The assertions made in this bulletin are preliminary and subject to the modifications of the final report, and fair criticism and recommendations are therefore invited in view of the possibly necessary revisions and corrections." The assertions of the New York labor statistician, Peck, a dissatisfied Democrat, were

thoroughly exploited by the Republicans on their posters
and in their assemblies. Peck was the object of an
outpouring of wrath on the part of the Democratic
politicians who proceeded against him in a genuine
American manner. The Election Committee of the
Democratic Party demanded an examination of Peck's
evidence and, when Peck refused such an examination or
the surrender of any documents, he was taken to court.
Before the court, Peck denied that the evidence was
public property and by clever legal stratagems succeeded
in having the legal proceedings adjourned until after
the elections. Various persons asserted or wanted to
prove that the evidence had been burned upon Peck's
instructions. However, eight days after the elections,
the judge decided that Peck was not culpable because the
law which had established the office did not designate
any place to keep documents or written depositions and
did not require an official to create such a place, nor
did the law obligate an official to preserve any
statistics except those that are contained in his annual
report to the legislature.

Peck and Porter worked in vain as was shown by the
presidential elections, but their good will was
recognized, their dubious statistics made use of, and
their achievements by far surpassed by the then (not reelected) President Harrison who, in his final message to
congress on December 6th, 1892, stated as follows:

> " . . . I can say with satisfaction that the
> general condition of the United States as far as
> trade and industry are concerned is highly
> favorable. A comparison with the favorable
> periods of our country will show, I believe, that
> such a high degree of prosperity and such a
> general enjoyment of the comforts of life have
> never been before such a part of our people's
> lives. . ."

He then quotes the total sums of the census
bulletin concerning factory statistics in 75 important
cities in the country and adds:

> "The income from wages not only shows an
> increase of the total sum, but also a per capita
> increase from $386 during the year 1880 to $547 in
> the year 1890 or an increase of 41.47%."

Of the saving banks' deposits, he states:

> "It is estimated that 90% of these deposits
> are the savings of wage earners."

Furthermore, he says:

"Never before was work so abundant or the
wages so adequate, whether one measures them with
the value of money or the purchasing power."

And he concludes:

"If people here are unhappy with their
condition, if they believe that wages and prices,
the fruits of honest work are inadequate, they
should remember that there is no country in the
world where these conditions, which seem to be so
depressing to them, would not be regarded in the
most favorable light. The English agriculturist
would love to exchange his income with that of the
American farmer, and the workers at Manchester
(England) would love to trade their wages with
their colleagues in Fall River (America)."

The highest official of the country quotes reports
which the census bureau itself calls "preliminary and
subject to modification," and he cites statistics from
Peck's work, whose documentary evidence the latter
refused to produce and/or destroy. The comments about
the saving deposits and about the situation of the
workers at Manchester and at Fall River have been
thoroughly refuted for the most part twenty years ago in
the reports of the statistical labor office in
Massachusetts (and the two officials of the bureau at
that time, Oliver and McNeill, were fired for just that
reason). The comparison between the English and
American agriculturists is given the lie by the
thousands of deserted farms of the New England states as
well as the threatening movement of the small farmers in
the West and South of the United States. The most
outrageous part of the U.S. President's remarks was his
extravagant praise of the well-being and prosperity of
the country and the labor market in the year of
Homestead, Coeur D'Alene, Buffalo, Tennessee, etc. If
one believes the statements of the President, then the
workers at the above-named places must have done very
well and they must have initiated the battles during
which they risked their lives, livelihood and liberty,
just for the fun of it!
The earlier description of the events in Tennessee,
etc., and the defeats which the workers suffered there,
was accompanied by the remark that even these defeats
can mean the salvation of the labor movement if the big
labor unions learn a lesson from it and draw closer
together in order to advance in a common front. Great
hopes were, therefore, placed upon the annual
conventions of the Knights of Labor (K. of L.) and the
American Federation of Labor (A.F.L.) which met during
November and December of 1892. These hopes were
bitterly disappointed.

The convention of the Knights of Labor met on
November 15th in St. Louis, and the official organ of
the Knights, in its last pre-convention issue on
November 10th, threw a bucket of ice-cold water on the
previously-mentioned hopes with the following words:
"During former sessions, much time and thought was
devoted to the attempt to discover the means whereby
organizations which mainly pursued similar aims like
ours could be dissuaded from behaving in an unfriendly
or perhaps even hostile manner towards us. It is
worthwhile to consider whether the time and the thought
along those lines has not really been a waste." The
Grand Master Workman of the order, Mr. I. V. Powderly,
goes even further in his annual message to the
convention, but prefaces it with a few diplomatic
phrases: " . . . It is a fact that there are too many
labor organizations which fight for hegemony . . . the
trend of the labor movement seems to be towards
isolation while the tendency of the opposing force,
capitalism, is towards concentration . . . something
should be done in order to remove this evil . . . a
friendly hand should be extended to all those that work
on this." He then continues: "There is no reason why
every branch of labor should not be incorporated under
the banner of this order, etc." At a subsequent place
in his speech he states: "We must make an effort to
come closer to the other industrial unions and as a step
in that direction, I recommend that we will meet in the
future at the same time and at the same place as the
Farmers' Alliance."--which means with the organization
of the small farmers of the West and the South. As for
the rest, this man devoted a lot of space and words to
the ballot reform, i.e., the safeguarding of the ballot
box, the referendum and immigration.
     As far as the immigration question is concerned, he
stated among other things that he had advocated the
limitation of immigration already six years ago and that
he had since come to the conclusion that an even
stricter exclusion of immigrants must be demanded. He
then continued: "We may be able to put into effect laws
to shorten the working hours in every state, put up wage
scales in every state, issue protective tariffs until
there is a complete prohibition of the import of foreign
industrial products but, as long as the flood of
immigration continues in an unbroken stream, the
shortening of the work week is an illusion, the wage
scale is uncertain, and there is no protection for
American labor since the condition of the American
laborer would not be raised above that of his brother
who has lived for centuries under monarchical
mismanagement. Your Grand Master Workman is not afraid
to state that he supports the total exclusion of all
immigrants who are not self-sustaining."

The "approach to other labor organizations"
receives a very special twist by the recommendation of
the Grand Master Workman to rescind the syndicate treaty
between the miners of both tendencies (open and secret),
a treaty which for several years accomplished much that
was positive.

The convention turned over the dissolution of the
above-mentioned syndicate in a somewhat modified form to
the executive committee, rejected after an intense
debate a declaration of war against the American
Federation of Labor (A.F.L.), ordered the introduction
of a certain kind of referendum for the administration
of the order, rejected the exclusion of paid politicians
from offices of the order, authorized the creation of a
Knights of Labor cadet corps (consisting of 10 to 18
year old children of members), recommended the
acquisition of a kind of uniform for the Knights of
Labor, lifted the boycott against the Third Avenue
Railroad in New York, and declared a boycott against the
Second Avenue Railroad. Resolutions were drawn up
against the Pinkertons, for a more popular National
Guard system, against sweat shops, for initiative and
referendum, for free silver coinage, and against the
immigration of persons who are not self-sustaining.
Furthermore it was decided to sell the expensive order
building in Philadelphia and perhaps to move the seat of
the administration. Powderly, though not without
opposition, was again elected as Grand Master Workman.

The second larger union, the American Federation of
Labor (A.F.L.) held its annual convention from December
12th until the 17th at Philadelphia. Present were 89
delegates that represented 67 different organizations
and 229,800 members. The well-written annual report
(message) of president Gompers gave a succinct survey of
the outstanding events of the year (Homestead, Coeur
D'Alene, Buffalo, Tennessee) and emphasized the increase
in capitalist infringements. As antidote, only the
strengthening and expansion of the organizations was
recommended, and against the misuse of the National
Guard, only its reorganization on a more popular basis
was recommended. The report opposes unlimited
immigration, the proceedings of the Knights of Labor in
regards to the establishment of better relations with
the American Federation of Labor, the closing of the
World Fair at Chicago on Sundays; it supports new
efforts for the attainment of the eight-hour day, etc.
The reports of the secretary and treasurer showed an
annual income of $25,990.87 and expenditures of
$18,324.69 and a present balance of $7,666.18.

Of the convention's decisions, the following are
worth mentioning: the strikers at Homestead were to be
given a thousand dollars, those in Coeur D'Alene five
hundred, and the ones in Tennessee also five hundred in
support money; a general vote was to be held over the

question whether a war chest of five times one hundred
thousand dollars should be established. Decisions were
made against the so-called philanthropy of Jewish aid
organizations and the Baron Hirsch funds, for the
pardoning of Fielden, Schwab and Neebe, for the
expropriation of the railways and transport companies,
for the women's right to vote, for direct legislation,
for compulsory education, and for a vivid enlightenment
and propaganda campaign. A number of boycotts were
declared, a decision about independent political
activity was rejected, the old officials were reelected,
and it was decided to hold the next convention at
Chicago on December 11th, 1893.

A mutual rapprochement of these large unions was
out of the question as far as both of these
organizations were concerned. There were a few phrases
about brotherhood and such things in the documents that
were designed for the public, but no deeds followed
these words so that one might almost get the idea that
the daily events, the suppressions, the privations and
mistreatments of the workers, had passed unnoticed by
these labor organizations if a whole series of events of
this past year had not obviously shown the opposite:
the undeniable symptoms of a very spirited feeling of
solidarity among the workers. It emerged rather clearly
that the leaders and officials of these unions must
largely be blamed for these quarrels.

During its session of 1892, the legislature of the
State of New York passed a law against the so-called
sweating system, against the sweat shops, and the
legislature of Massachusetts, too, took measures to
remove or to limit the worst evils of the wide-spread
home industry. Boston pursued a very intense campaign
against the just-mentioned system, but when the factory
inspector of the State of New York was approached about
carrying out this law, the gentleman declared that his
office had no authority to carry it out. The law, so he
said, states that the mayor is permitted to appoint
officials to carry it out, but it does not specify which
mayor, and no means are provided to pay these officials.
The law would probably be declared unconstitutional
anyway.

At the last congress of the Social Science
Association (which corresponds somewhat to the Verein
für Sozialpolitik in Germany) at Saratoga, New York, in
September of last year, the then Chief of the
Statistical Labor Bureau of Massachusetts, H. S. Wadlin,
gave the following information about the sweating
system, especially in Massachusetts: "The system is
primarily used in the clothing industry whose annual
products have a value of 25 million, of which 90% are
manufactured under the sweatshop system. Boston
constituted half, New York a sixth (?), Maine a quarter,
and the rest were shared by New Hampshire and New

Jersey. The quantity of work that is sent by Boston manufacturers for completion to New York increases all the time. Persons of foreign extraction form the majority of the workers. Of 1147 persons who were investigated, 448 were Jews, 249 Americans, 215 Italians, 16 Irish, 13 Portuguese and 6 German. Jews predominate among the contractors because 931 workers (out of the above-mentioned number) were employed by Jewish contractors. In order to make a profit, the contractor gives to certain people (namely the sub-contractor), instead of wages, a certain percentage of the daily rate of work that they squeeze out of their slaves. In many cases, piece work predominates, and hours of labor are disregarded. The laborer's family eats, sleeps and works in the same room so that the employer is able to save the rent for the place of work and does not have to worry about factory regulations. In New York, the sweat shops are supposed to be only in their initial stages (?) and they are supposed to be far behind those in Massachusetts." Commenting about his own description of the conditions accompanying this system, Mr. Wadlin states at another place in his lecture: "The contract system itself is not really so reprehensible. The accompanying evils only enter upon the scene when the unscrupulous contractors take over the work with substandard wages." Oh, yes, it is the bourgeois conscience which produces the unscrupulousness of the contractors. American citizens boast of themselves as being respectful of the law, or law-abiding. This is most amply demonstrated, for example, by the fact that last year, at the beginning of September, twenty-four underage children were found to work in a single factory in New York.

During the Autumn of 1892, various large strikes took place like the miners' strike in the soft coal region near Pittsburgh, the strike of the coat workers at Brooklyn (New York) and the strike of the construction workers in the City of New York. The first named strike was ended after a long duration by a meagre settlement, the second was terminated in a similar fashion, and the third concluded with a defeat of the powerful Construction Workers' Union of the City of New York.

New Orleans, the large trading city at the mouth of the Mississippi, was the scene of an interesting battle: the experimental station for the general strike. How the feeling of solidarity there began to stir at an early time has been described previously. The task of organizing the workers there, regardless of the differences of nationality, color, language or sex, had succeeded in New Orleans to a great degree so that, during the spring of 1892, the labor council of the city (the assembly of the unions' delegates), consisting of 61 different unions, made an intensive effort to attain

better working conditions, wages and working hours. Its
chief effort, however, was directed towards uniting as
many people as possible in each field of work. The
presidential election year seemed to hold particularly
good prospects for success. The workers in the large
storage houses and the loaders of freight cars demanded
from the employers that they only employ union members,
and when the employers (mostly of the great trading
firms) rejected this request, the workers began to
strike on October 24th. The labor council made common
cause with the workers and, in order to cause the
employers to yield, they declared several days later the
general strike. With the exception of certain workers
who are involved in the shipment of cotton, almost all
workers of the city went on strike and the bourgeois
minds were seized with an indescribable panic. The
bourgeoisie would have loved to go on the attack, but
there were too many workers and, besides, there were
presidential elections on November 9th. The governor,
mayor, and police chief all put their heads together but
did not dare to do anything until the elections were
over. The day after the elections, however, the
National Guard was rapidly called up, the strikers were
intimidated and kept away at a respectful distance while
scabs were brought in. The strike was at an end and
"order" had been restored.

On November 20th, after a duration of more than 20
weeks, the strike at Homestead was declared as having
been terminated by the association of iron and steel
workers. But with the conclusion of the strike, the
court indictments and trials of the participants really
got underway, so that by December there were about 200
workers either under arrest or out on bail. A justice
of the supreme court of Pennsylvania, who regarded the
accusations against the strikers of insurrection, arson
and murder as too lenient and insufficient, came down
from his high seat and assumed the position of a simple
justice of the peace (which he was legally entitled to
do) and announced the following new verdict: the
strikers of Homestead had committed treason against the
state by their memorable fight. The merits of the man
were rewarded, because shortly thereafter, he resigned
from the bench in order to assume a most lucrative
position with a railroad association. The first murder
trial against one of the strikers named Critchlow ended
on November 23rd with the accused being freed by the
jury of all charges, much to the great and undisguised
disgust of the presiding judge. The later murder trial
against H. O'Donnell, one of the Homestead people, also
ended with an acquittal. But at the same time, the
brutal guard officers who had tortured the guard
soldier, Jems, too, were acquitted. The bourgeois
conscience works at times in unpredictable ways!

Already at the end of September, four Coeur D'Alene miners had been sentenced from 15 months to 2 years' imprisonment for conspiracy, but they have appealed their sentences to the Supreme Court of the United States. On November 16th, the four and a half months old martial law at Coeur D'Alene was lifted. High treason and martial law, does this not sound familiar to the German workers?

Chapter III: Endnotes

[1]Not because of opposition to capitalist exploitation, but because these statistics glorified the protective tariff regime of the Republicans.

Domestic Market—Financial Crisis of 1893— Silver and Tariff Legislation—Sugar and Tariff Legislation—Sugar Trust

The Republican President Harrison in his farewell message (December 1892) ascribed the general prosperity of the country to the "McKinley Tariffs" and described the well being of the workers in glowing colors. He could not help, however, to give the dissatisfied elements, whose presence he could not deny after Homestead, Coeur D'Alene, etc., the same advice that the German emperor had once bluntly given--namely, that they should shake the dust off their feet. His Democratic successor, President Cleveland, in his inaugural address of March 1893, on the other hand, could not stress enough how much the country, the industry, the great mass of the consumers, the little man, the farmer and the worker all wished for and needed a reduction of import duties so that industry may expand and consumers shop cheaply. President Cleveland also urgently recommended the cessation of monthly silver purchases by virtue of the Sherman Law (Sherman Bill) in order that the currency could attain a healthier basis. The economy, the development of industry as well as the labor movement ran their course without worrying in the least about the gentlemen Harrison and Cleveland. If Mr. Harrison had already been given the lie in advance during 1892 by the events of Homestead, Coeur D'Alene, Buffalo, Coal Creek, etc., the great activity of the most important organization of the country at the end of 1893 showed Mr. Cleveland, too, how little his words count and benefit.

The industry of this country has developed to an astonishing degree of efficiency. In many fields it has already surpassed Europe and, during the last years (1890-1893), it has produced and manufactured without a let-up and without regard to the market. The products must, however, find buyers, i.e., a market, and this

market is limited because it is a domestic market and
not even under the most favorable circumstances (not to
speak of unfavorable circumstances) can this domestic
market possibly absorb the mass of products that the
most important branches of America's big industry
(steel, cotton, etc.) throw on the market.

The numerically most important and most significant
consumers of the products that arrive on the market are
in the final analysis always the actual producers of
these wares: urban and rural workers in the factory and
on the fields, at the weaver's loom and in the coal
shaft. If these people possess the means that it takes
to cover the needs of their families, then "business is
flourishing" and the wares are transformed into money to
stimulate new production, provided they possess the best
quality of products: cheapness.

What means do the workers then possess at the
moment? As far as the industrial workers are concerned,
the answer is supplied by Homestead, Coeur D'Alene,
Buffalo, etc., that is, by the wage battles of the
textile, construction and mine workers as well as the
workers in almost all branches of industry. Only a
cold-blooded nonentity (as the widow of the deceased
James G. Blaine called him) and an insolent ignoramus
like Benjamin Harrison could, in view of these battles,
dare to speak of unparalleled prosperity. The
industrial workers of the United States have, for a long
time, been pushed below their customary standard of
living, and they are no longer able to fulfill their
needs in the accustomed way. A large part of the
domestic market is damaged thereby, and the well-known
and popular method of producing ever cheaper goods fails
to work here because of the limitation of the market.
Industry is locked into a vicious circle. Lower prices
of products seldom go hand in hand with high wages.
Thus if one reduces the wages, one also reduces the
ability of the workers to consume. The workers rebel,
so one imports cheaper workers from Italy, Poland,
Hungary, Russia, or China; but this hardly helps to
revive the market, because the Slovaks or Huns (they are
preferably referred to as Huns), Italians, etc., consume
very little, help the internal market very little and,
which is worse, finally they, too, become rebellious and
snarl at their exploiters, as happened, for example, in
the coke district.

Oh, no! The means of the industrial workers are
totally insufficient to revive the internal market.

If American industry today experiences unfavorable
sales as far as the industrial workers are concerned,
things are even worse as far as the producers of raw
materials and foodstuffs and the workers in agriculture
and on the cotton fields etc. are concerned. On the
world market there is a veritable embarras de richesse
as far as most raw materials and agricultural products

go. Wheat, cotton, corn, etc. have been planted in such
quantities that their price often does not even meet the
cost of producing them. The farmers of the West and the
Mid-West of the United States have often used corn as
fuel when corn did not bring acceptable prices. R.
Meyer, who is certainly an expert on agriculture,
writes: "In the long run the independent farmer will
not be able to deliver wheat at 50 cents a bushel."
Already last year in Kansas, a farmer complained that he
could get at the most 48 cents for a bushel of wheat and
during this year (1894) the farmers from Dakota and
Canada to Kansas receive only 45 cents and sometimes as
little as 43 cents so that in many parts of the West,
the farmers are feeding the wheat to their animals. In
Orange, Ulster and other counties that constitute the
milk chambers of New York, the farmers receive at the
most 1 1/2 cents for a quart (about a litre) of milk and
in Washington County, probably the most fertile district
of Wisconsin not far from Milwaukee, the farmers get 2
cents per pound of milk, i.e., 1 and 1 1/2 cents per
quart. These are authenticated statistics from real
life.
     Naturally, the profits from the small farmer's
crops and the wages of rural laborers have become so
small that the larger part of the country's population
is hardly able to consume anymore and, therefore, is of
little use to the domestic market.
     As shown above, as far as the domestic market is
concerned, the circumstances are unfavorable for the
sale of products but even if the circumstances were most
favorable, the domestic market just is not big enough
anymore for American industry. "Man must face the
hostile world," states Schiller in his song of songs of
the petit-bourgeoisie, and the upper bourgeoisie of the
United States has created a variant of this song and the
industrial bourgeoisie of Europe by exclaiming: "The
products must face the world market" if we are to
maintain our position as exploiters par excellence. We
have lots of capital, we have innumerable skilled
workers, we are protected against having to pay high
wages by a large industrial reserve army that can be
enlarged at any time, we have machinery that is admired
in the entire world, we have excellent technical
equipment and seemingly inexhaustible natural resources.
What is still lacking? Cheap raw materials. Thus let
us do away with protective tariffs on raw materials and
the world and the world market will belong to us! Thus
think the big industrialists of the United States and
sometimes they clearly say so, as for example, Mr.
Carnegie, but the opposition to it has by no means been
broken and finds strong support among the native
Americans' peculiar clinging to old traditions. Just as
Marx, forty years ago, predicted for old Europe, the
devastating competition of the new world, so Engels

prophesied more than eight years ago to the American
supporters of protective tariffs, the impending advent
of free trade.

In anticipation of the coming changes, the last
Republican protective tariff congress of the United
States had done everything possible to make future
change in the tariff legislation more difficult by
increasing the budget to such heights that it was
labeled the congress of the billions. The country's
banking institutes, which are all private (even though
nine-tenths of them are deceptively named "national
banks") followed the tempting example of the legislators
of the country and created anticipatory bank-rate
rebates in expectation of the new era. When in
connection with this several irregularities ended with
the well-known custom of a Canadian escape,[1] several
money institutions, savings banks, etc., had shut down
shortly after President Cleveland's inauguration. In
the wake of this, a boundless distrust seized the so-
called business community and the Philistines, a
distrust which was reinforced by a simultaneous export
of gold to Europe (which, however, did not last very
long) and a lack of small denomination paper money. The
large, solid banks became very careful and, for a while,
even paid only with deposit receipts and clearing-house
slips and refused to invest in the manufacturers' bills
of exchange. Many of the big industrialists were forced
to close their factories because of this lack of money
and others, who were not thus pressed, found it
convenient to do likewise or, what happened most
frequently, they used this opportunity to carry out
significant wage reductions.

All of this was happening during the exultation and
the conceited self-adulation of the Chicago Worlds Fair.

The constantly increasing unemployment, the wage
reductions and the sufferings they caused to the working
class did not in the least touch the world of the
officials, politicians and office holders, but the
exploitation was temporarily disturbed and restricted
and, therefore, the bourgeois world was screaming for
help in Washington. The short-sighted Cleveland promised
help by calling a special session of congress in August
1893 in order to revoke the Sherman Bill.

The Sherman Law, named after its author, was
designed in 1890 in order to allure the silver
sweethearts and small farmers. It orders the monthly
purchase of 4,500,000 ounces of silver at the market
price in order to coin silver dollars, "the dollars of
our fathers." Since these silver dollars, because of
the drop in the price of silver on the world market,
were constantly losing in value, and since their weight
felt too heavy in the bourgeois pockets, congress
simultaneously ordered the issuance of paper money in
place of the silver dollars while the latter were

stored, untouched in the vaults and mints of the United
States, protected from devaluation by the constituting
currency. Nobody wanted to have these silver dollars or
to take them in payment, and the situation reached a
point where the government did not possess enough
treasuries and fire and theft-proof vaults to store the
glittering metal. This plethora of silver, which daily
became less valuable (particularly since the cessation
of silver coinage in India) and which was continued[2]
solely in the interest of a few silver barons and in
the interests of a few small states, the so-called
silver states, required great monthly expenditures at a
time when the budget was threatening to come close to a
deficit. All of this was supposed to have caused the
financial collapse which was to be alleviated by the
repeal of the Sherman Law!
     Congress met on August 6th, 1893, and chattered
away for nearly three months before the law was revoked.
     During the congressional debate over the Sherman
Law as well as after the repeal of the law, the business
situation and the labor market of the country grew
steadily worse. The number of bankruptcies reached an
unheard of height and the army of the unemployed had
swollen mightily when congress, after a short recess in
December of last year (1893), met again and very soon
started a debate about the so-called tariff, i.e., the
customs legislation. In the course of the winter (1893-
94), the situation of the industrial unemployed (the
workers in industry who had been thrown out into the
street) grew worse and led to significant demonstrations
in the larger cities of the country. The unemployment
in the Mid-West and West of the country found expression
in the march of Coxey and his followers to Washington
where they pounded in vain on the doors of congress, the
"people's representation." The miners rebelled and laid
down their work in many states under threatening
circumstances. The coke workers fought energetically
and desperately for their existence and finally there
occurred the big rebellion of the Allied Railway
Workers, the American Railway Union against Pullman, a
strike which stirred up the entire country. But
nothing, absolutely nothing, disturbed the gentlemen
people's representatives in their barter deals. Nothing
interrupted their stupid and hypocritical babbling that
lasted from the beginning of the winter 1893/94 until
August 13th, 1894.
     The new tariff law is a monster whose father is the
corruption and the obvious venality of a great number of
senators and representatives and whose mother is the
cowardice and the lack of character by the other
gentlemen people's representatives and the bourgeois
press. Matchless even for the United States is the
proven (verified by documents and undisputed witnesses)
corruptibility of various influential senators, and just

as matchless is the brazen attitude of the bribed
subjects and the whitewashing of their actions--about
which more will be related below.

The main battle in congress was not concerned with
the tariffs on raw materials but the tariff on sugar
which is demanded by the sugar trust, a cartel formed
several years ago by the large sugar refineries of the
country. This sugar trust is at the moment, except for
the Standard Oil Company, the most important and
influential trust in the United States, if not the
world. It possesses a fabulous amount of capital issued
in shares of stock, and it makes no secret of the fact
(which certainly does weigh on its conscience) that it
uses huge amounts of money to influence the legislatures
of the different states, especially the national
legislature, the congress, to attain votes favorable to
its interests.

When the scandal became too great to be covered up
any longer, the Senate, because of its honor or shame,
appointed an investigation committee during whose
sessions it was revealed that during the consultations
about the sugar tariff, various senators had made
marvellous profits with shares of the sugar trust. The
committee, however, came out with a general whitewash
report by giving as reason for its inconclusive findings
the fact that its main witness had refused to testify
and another witness had fled to Canada. Nevertheless,
the committee could not help but state casually that:

> "they take occasion to strongly deprecate the
> importunity and pressure to which congress and its
> members are subjected by the representatives of
> great industrial combinations, whose enormous
> wealth tends to suggest undue influence and to
> create in the public mind a demoralizing belief in
> the existence of corrupt politics . . . "

The committee reports "that Senator Pherson
(Democrat) and Senator Quay (Republican) possessed sugar
shares and dealt with them during the consultations
about the tariff law but that they divested themselves
of these shares before the vote." The committee was
shown a photographic copy of a large order of sugar
shares for Senator Camden and while the execution of
this order was contested "he (Senator Camden) refuses to
swear positively that the order does not contain his
signature." The two Republican members of the
committtee report in a supplementary appendix: "It was
admitted and proven by the sworn testimonies of every
witness who testified that the present form of the sugar
tariff is the one that was desired by the
representatives of the refineries or the sugar trust."
The president and several members of the administrative
council of the "sugar trust" testified that the trust

had made significant contributions to the campaign funds of both bourgeois parties, to the Democrats in Democratic states and to the Republicans in Republican states. They refused to reveal the amount of the contributions (it should be mentioned here that it was publicly asserted in the entire press that during the last presidential elections in 1892 the sugar trust donated 500,000 dollars to the election committee of the Democratic Party. This assertion remains uncontested). At the end of its report, however, the investigation committee states brazenly that it could not state that any senator let himself be influenced in a corrupt or illegal way during the consultations about the tariff law "and no attempt was made to influence the legislation in this way."

The sugar tariff remained, the tariffs on raw materials (except for wool) were not rescinded, and the new tariff law (the Gorman Tariff) came into force on August 28th without the signature of the president.

Chapter IV: Endnotes

[1]Our great swindlers, embezzling bank presidents, cashiers, state and country treasurers, usually flee across the border to Canada for their personal safety and the safety of their loot.

5
Judicial Power and Practice in the United States, 1894–1895

Already 45 years ago in his book <u>The 18th Brumaire of Louis Napoleon</u>, Karl Marx described the bourgeois republic of the United States of North America as the conservative way of life of bourgeois society, and Friedrich Engels wrote some time ago: ". . . in other respects, the Americans have for some time proven to the European world that the bourgeois republic is the republic of the capitalist businessmen, where politics is simply a business transaction like any other."

The workers of the old world still frequently hear the praise and glory of the new world, and the United States is presented to them as an exemplary model of undiluted democracy, a commonwealth of free and independent burghers. The "burghers" (bourgeois) rule here indeed as in no other country in the world. Neither monarchical nor feudal nor clerical institutions limit the "bourgeois" call to exploit, and "bourgeois" are all institutions and characteristics here. Truly bourgeois is their conceit, truly bourgeois is their lust for exploitation, and truly bourgeois is their brutality vis-a-vis the weaker people, etc. Much praised and partially imitated is the famous division of power in the United States, the so-called mutual control of the executive, legislative and judicial functions. They are all of a bourgeois nature. It has previously been shown how the executive and legislative powers are purely bourgeois, and this will be shown frequently in subsequent chapters. How the judicial power is constituted and how it is even more bourgeois in nature than the other two put together will now be illustrated.

Bourgeois property is protected by laws[1] for whose
preservation and interpretation courts are maintained
whose personnel, with few exceptions, comes from the
profession of lawyers and jurists. Since every state
(there are now 45 of them) has its own law code, while a
great number of litigations take place in several states
at once, it can be imagined what incredible numbers of
lawyers are needed and employed. The lawyers in this
country constitute a prominent profession. Lawyers
nearly control all legislatures just by virtue of their
numerical strength, since at least two-thirds of all
legislatures are controlled by lawyers. Among certain
strata of the population exist strong antipathies
towards lawyers, and it is for this reason that the
constitution of the Knights of Labor does not permit any
lawyers to enter the order.

Most judges, as mentioned before, come from the
ranks of the lawyers, but the process of nominating them
(with the exception of nominations to the federal
courts) is not at all uniform. In many states the
justices of the various courts are elected by the
people, in other states they are appointed by the
governor or the legislature, etc. In order to give an
example, let me describe the procedure in the states of
New York and New Jersey: in New York all judges to the
higher courts are elected by the people, and in the
county districts even the justices of the peace. In the
City of New York, however, all the magistrates are
appointed by the mayor. In New Jersey all judges of the
higher courts are appointed by the governor with the
participation of the legislature; the justices of the
peace, however, are elected by the people, etc. The
tenure of judges usually runs from four to fifteen
years, but there are appointments for life up to a
certain age limit. The salary of a judge of the higher
courts runs between $3,000 to $10,000 a year, while the
justices of the peace, the poor devils of the people,
receive nothing but their fees.

Besides the laws of the 45 individual states, there
are also general, i.e., federal laws and laws for the
territories, and consequently there are also federal
courts and federal judges. The whole territory of the
United States is divided into federal districts, each of
which is presided over by a federal judge. Above all,
as the highest authority and the highest body of judges,
stands the Supreme Court of the United States. All
federal judges, federal attorneys and federal marshals
are appointed by the president with the advice of the
senate. The judges are given a lifetime appointment.

The people, as such, do not participate in the
filling of the offices, nor do they exercise the
slightest influence when it comes to the judicial
appointments. This, as well as the exclusive
jurisdiction of federal courts in all interstate trade

and lawsuits must be kept in mind.

When in the 1870's, the railroad companies gained and exercised such significant influence over legislation, the petit-bourgeoisie and the rural west let out a loud scream and demanded the restoration of the people's power. They saw to it that Congress appointed the so-called Inter-State Commission to regulate the railroads. This commission, which was originally designed (as just reported) to protect the people, has long since been seized with trickery by the railroad companies and has become one of its best means of exploitation. It has been changed into a firm protective barrier against the claims and demands of the employees and workers, and against the wishes and needs of the general public. The only merit of this office is its issuance of an annual statistical report about the railroad system of the United States.

As stated above, the justice positions in the individual states are occupied by members of the bar, and the appointments are almost always made with the advice of the bar association of the respective district, without whose approval appointments and selections almost never occur. The federal judges are appointed from the same circles and it is, therefore, hardly surprising that the federal justices have almost no (and the state judges extremely little) connections with the real people but all the more ties with the influential bourgeois circles of the politicians, etc.

Thus far the organization of the courts and the nominations to the judicial positions have been briefly described, and it would be useful to describe, too, the jury system as well as the selection of juries in the United States. Due to the lack of space, this cannot be done now. Just how the jury system and the jury selection are handled has been shown by the trial against A. Spiess and comrades, and reference should also be made in this connection to the memorandum of Governor Altgeld on the occasion of the pardoning of Schwab, Fielden and Neebe.

Very interesting to read, and also instructive, are the decisions, judgments and actions of bourgeois justices in all cases that concern workers and their endeavors, especially if these workers have committed the crime of not having been born in the United States. Here is a limited selection from the states of Pennsylvania, New York and New Jersey.

Berkman, who had made the attempt on the life of the vice-king of Homestead, Frick, was condemned to 22 years in the penitentiary at Pittsburgh, Pennsylvania. The judge who was angry that he could not give Berkman more than 12 to 15 years for the bungled assassination attempt, used cumulative method and added to the attempt on the person, the attempt on the home, i.e., illegal entry into a stranger's house, and thus raised the

punishment to the desired severity. Bauer and Nolde,
two workers who could not be charged with anything
except that one had given shelter to Berkman and the
other had accompanied him on a walk that passed Frick's
office, were given 5 to 8 years of penitentiary at the
same city of Pittsburgh. In New York, Emma Goldmann was
supposed to have given incendiary speeches in the German
language at a gathering of unemployed. This claim was
made by a police informer who did not even understand
German correctly, yet Emma Goldmann was given a year in
jail because of his testimony. A lot of rough action
occurred during a strike of silk weavers at Paterson,
New Jersey during the spring of 1894. Threatening
letters were sent and even a bomb was found. The
gentlemen factory owners became worried, and a number of
mostly German workers were arrested and put on trial.
During the trial it was revealed that an agent
provocateur had made use of the excitement surrounding
the strike to show a few naive workers the preparation
and use of dynamite and to recommend its usage. The
stool pigeon, of course, went scot-free. One of the
workers received 6 years (5 years for a bomb that had
not exploded and 1 year for a minatory letter), another
worker was given 6 months because he had translated a
threatening letter, and several others each got 1 year
because of the mistreatment of scabs and because of
conspiracy. The spirit of dirty partisanship and vain
ignorance that pervades most occupants of American
juridical offices is best illustrated by the following
excerpt from the final speech of the judge at Paterson:

"Most, if not all persons that participated
in the violent actions are of foreign origin and
are blindly ignorant about the rights and
privileges of free American citizens or they
deliberately disregard them. Every person in this
free country has the constitutional right to work
for anyone that employs him or to give up a job if
he chooses to do so, but nobody has the right to
force upon that person one or the other. The
employer has the right to hire people and to have
them work for him under such conditions and for
such wages as he and his employees mutually agreed
upon. If he so desires, he may dismiss his
employees and shut his factory. Whoever forcibly
interferes with this process is guilty of a crime
and should be summarily punished. Workers have
the right to organize and to form associations and
to achieve an increase in wages by peaceful means
as well as to improve their situation in other
ways. But when they turn to violence to attain
their goals, destroy property or attack their co-
workers (colleagues), they violate the fundamental
principles of our free government and are not

worthy of the American civil right. A government
that has been instituted by the people and for the
people is obligated to maintain its unrestricted
sovereignty. Its defeat would mean the perdition
of the entire people. The open or secret
principles of anarchy or socialism, according to
which these law breakers seem to have acted, will
never be permitted to seize a foothold in this
free country. . . . "

These samples may suffice for the time being as far
as the state courts and the foreign born are concerned.
They clearly show that the United States, too, have
their "Brausewetter." They are equal to the Berliner as
far as prejudice is concerned but the Americans far
surpass him when it comes to a lack of logic and
education.

It was stated above that the railroad companies
very soon transformed the Inter State Commission, which
supposedly had been created for the protection of the
public from the infringements of the railroads, into one
of the best weapons against the public, especially
against the workers. The large railroads of this
country cross several, sometimes many, states, each of
which has its special legislation and judicial code,
which, according to all its Philistines, ought to be
maintained at all costs. As soon as the railroads came
into conflict with their employees and called upon the
aid of the county and state authorities against the
miscreants, the aid which was rendered most willingly
did not go further than the boundary of the country or
the state. What the bourgeois authorities decided upon
in Buffalo, New York, was not valid in Toledo, Ohio, and
what was carried out in Milwaukee, Wisconsin, was not
applicable to Detroit, Michigan, etc. To overcome these
hindrances cost the train companies a lot of time and
money. As soon as the Inter State Commission was put
into action, these difficulties were removed at one
stroke because now these matters came before federal
authorities and federal courts whose jurisdiction was
not limited by state or county borders. Whenever the
railway companies were perturbed about the
insubordination of its subjects, an obsequious federal
judge could be found to do the bidding of the company.

Bourgeois cleverness, which is derived from the
exploitative instinct, was displayed by the federal
authorities and justices when they assumed a hostile
position vis-a-vis the workers and employees of the
railroads by a seemingly genuine American
mercantilistic-juridical maneuver which allows the
railroad companies who do not fulfill their financial
obligations and are unable to pay interest on their
loans to declare bankruptcy before an appropriate
federal court. The federal judge then appoints a

receiver who has behind him the full authority of the
federal government and who is entitled to call to his
aid the federal authorities and federal troops.
Insurrection against a receiver then was and is regarded
as insurrection against the federal government, if not
high treason. What tremendous concessions are made here
to the exploitative instincts and how significant this
whole process has become may be seen from the fact that
by the summer of 1894, the major part of the Western and
Pacific railroads is in receivership and administered by
the federal government.^{2}

The federal judges obtained work and, corresponding
to their higher rank, they also tried to attain higher
and greater achievements than the state judges. Here
are a few examples.

A federal judge at New Orleans, almost
shamefacedly, took the lead in the decisions and
verdicts at the beginning of 1893, by declaring the
previously described general strike at New Orleans
(October and November 1892) as illegal (after it had run
its course) as much as it had interfered with inter-
state communications, i.e., the trade and traffic
between the individual states. The decision came post
festum since the accused object no longer existed, but a
precedent had been created and the majority of cases in
American courts are decided according to precedent, and
the lawyers here run and chase after precedents like
crazy.

Much more important for its consequences was the
juridical intervention in the battle of the railroad
employees against the Ann Arbor Railroad during March of
1893 because in this instance the superbly organized,
but extremely conservative, Brotherhood of Locomotive
Engineers stood at the center of the fight; and, for the
first time in such cases, a federal judge of the United
States made use of the now favorite and notorious
injunction which forbade the strikers to continue their
strike. The case created a big stir, but in view of the
well-known conservative character of the brotherhood and
Mr. Arthur, there were not any negative consequences for
the accused who were let off with a nominal fine.

A federal judge in Georgia must have appeared like
a blackbird to his fellow judges when he ordered the
receiver of a railroad to pay the railroad workers union
wages, i.e., wages which had been determined in
negotiations with the employees' union. The example was
not contagious because an adjacent federal judge ordered
his receiver to do just the opposite. The remainder of
1893 offered nothing special in regard to the federal
courts. The decisions of Taft and Ricks in the Ann
Arbor case must yet take effect.

They did influence the federal judges and spurred
them on to imitate them and to surpass them during the
following year, i.e., during the current year 1894. The

poor Coxeyites were the first ones to feel them when
they were unpleasantly disturbed during their strange
pilgrimage to Washington by regular federal troops (sent
out because of federal courts' instructions) especially
in the Northwest, in the Dakotas, Montana, Idaho,
Wyoming, Nebraska, etc.

The federal judge Jenkins at Milwaukee, a man who
last winter was involved there in the collapse of a
bank, surpassed even the gentlemen Taft and Ricks by
forbidding (by way of injunctions), the strikers of a
railroad everything that might further their strike.
Many protests were raised, and the gentleman modified
his orders somewhat, but the whole matter (it was before
the great strike) was submitted to the House of
Representatives at Washington, which appointed a
committee to investigate the matter. The report of the
committee called the order of the judge absurd and
declared it null and void but, on the other hand, stated
that the man had acted without evil intent (?).

That was in May of this year. At the end of July,
the great Pullman Strike occurred, and now it was
raining injunctions, arrests, indictments and
convictions, especially because of contempt of court,
and always in the federal courts and for the most part
(this also happens in the US) because of an order from
above. Attorney-General Olney, a member of President
Cleveland's cabinet, ordered the United States attorney
at Chicago to appoint a grand jury in order to
investigate the incidents during the strike and to
indict the malcreants. The entire judicial apparatus is
working full blast and to the satisfaction of the
bourgeoisie and the authorities. Debs, the president of
the American Railway Union, and others were indicted,
arrested, and placed under high bail. At the time of
his arrest, Debs' papers and letters were ransacked and
seized. This, however, earned the over-zealous judge,
Grosscup (of whom more will be said in the future), a
reprimand which he accepted with a sour mien. More and
more new indictments were made, but when the first
indictment came up for trial, the trial, in spite of
sharp protests by the defense, was (on higher orders)
postponed until the autumn.

Not only in Chicago alone, but in all states and
territories (see more about this further on) where the
president proclaimed a state of siege--in North Dakota,
Montana, Idaho, Washington, Wyoming, Colorado,
California, Utah and New Mexico, as well as in many
others--the federal courts were working full time.
California was especially problematical because the
federal courts had a tough time there since they were
hardly respected. Many episodes from these trials could
be reported if space would only permit it. Let me
relate only two more cases which I will describe because
of the characteristic comments of the judges concerned.

Judge Taft, who last year during the Ann Arbor strike let the accused strikers off, has since then changed his attitude and has recently condemned a worker by the name of Phelan to six months in jail because of contempt of court. In his justification for his verdict he said among other things:

"This association (of the railway workers) is illegal because its purpose is to harm Pullman by the pressure which is put on the railroads . . . but it is also illegal because it seeks to carry out not a strike but a boycott, and a boycott is illegal even if it is free of violence; but even disregarding that, this association (to carry out the boycott) is illegal because it is a gigantic conspiracy which will lead to the starvation of the whole country, which can hardly be viewed as legal. . . ."

An achievement of the first order are the sincere and heartwarming remarks of Mr. Baker, the federal judge at Indianapolis, before whom the striking railway worker Murray stood, who was accused of contempt of court. The case was adjourned, but the judge could not help but pour out his bourgeois heart which led him to make the following comments:

"If we have an organization of men before us who are united in their desire to strike and to interfere with the actions of other men who want to work, whom they call scabs, then under such circumstances their simple call for them to join the strike must be viewed as a demand. If during a nocturnal hour a highwayman would appear and would say to me: Please, give me your billfold, I would be most grateful if you would do so, then I would still regard this request as a threat, even though it was said with great courtesy. If a member of a strike committee, with a group of embittered strikers behind it, says to a man who is in the service of the railroad: Well, do you not think that it would be nice if you, too, would join the strike?, then this request, too, must be viewed as a threat. It is the politeness of the highwaymen! People say: they are peaceful. Every intelligent person, however, knows that a strike would be meaningless if it would not be backed by violence. . . ."

Well, enough. From what has been reported (to which could be added a hundredfold more), the fact emerges clearly that the judicial power in the United States does not constitute any control over the executive and legislative branches but that it is simply an auxiliary force for the maintenance of power by the possessing classes, a complementary force for the other two factors designed for the better exploitation of the working class by the bourgeoisie, by the "free and independent"

citizens. The most striking proof for its genuine
bourgeois character and for the hostility towards the
workers by the local courts is supplied by the
interpretation of labor protection legislation by the
state and federal courts. Almost all such laws, as for
example the shortening of working hours, the limitation
of child labor, the protection of the lives and health
of workers, the abolition of the truck system, the
assurance of regular wages, the protection of women and
children--all such laws have been emasculated by the
courts of this land or they have been declared
unconstitutional.

Since injunctions have been mentioned so often,
here I would like to give the verbatim account of just
such an injunction. It was issued by Justice Dagro in
the City of New York on August 7th and confirmed eight
days later by a higher judge. It is directed at the
officials and all of the members (seven to eight
hundred) of a tailors' union, which had declared a
strike in thirteen tailor workshops in the City of New
York:

"The accused, their agents, servants,
deputies, allies and those persons hired by them
and each one of them individually, it is herewith
forbidden to interrupt, disturb or in any other
way, to interfere in the conduct and exercise of a
legal trade, business or profession of the
plaintiff, be it by a gathering or by loitering in
front of the place of business of the plaintiff or
in his immediate vicinity, or be it by the
organization or maintenance of a patrol, guard or
spy network by the placing or positioning of one
or more persons in front of or in the vicinity of
the plaintiff's business during business hours.
The accused are further forbidden by way of
printed matter or publications to interfere with
the business of the plaintiff, to lure away anyone
from the employment and work of the plaintiff or
by signs, words, stratagems, or any kind of
threat, to keep anyone from entering the service
of the plaintiff."

Chapter V: Endnotes

[1]It is true that there are laws for the protection of life and liberty, but one look into bourgeois legal books shows how small their number is in comparison to the laws designed to protect property.

[2]A single receiver controls a distance of 10,000 miles.

6
The Labor Movement, 1893 and 1894

It was reported earlier that the large labor organizations of the country, the Knights of Labor, the American Federation of Labor and the various unions of railway employees, hardly learned a lesson from the heavy fights of the year 1892 at Homestead, Coeur D'Alene, Buffalo and Tennessee. A few cheap declarations of sympathy and a little bit of money for the defense of the numerous victims was about all that the annual conventions of the Knights of Labor and the American Federation of Labor achieved during the autumn of 1892. When proposals were made to enter upon new paths and a little fresh current was stirring somewhere, all proposed innovations were quickly buried under the rubbish heap of the old routine, or they failed because of the unapproachability of the officials who had warmed their office seats for too long. Instead of fighting the common enemy, the large organizations made war upon each other and not only fought for each other's organizational territory but frequently even for the opportunity to work and to make a living. Especially egregious in these miserable quarrels were the tailor's cutters and other members of the clothing industry; and a by-no-means enviable role in these fraternal battles was played by the Jewish workers who, for several years, have totally monopolized several branches of the aforementioned industry. A similar fratricidal fight has been indulged in (one could almost say with a certain predilection) by the most recent unions which have existed only a few years, such as the bakers, the brewery workers, the waiters and barkeepers, etc. If one did not know and had it not been long ago proven that usually bourgeois entrepreneurs and politicians have a direct hand in these events, one would think that the participants enjoyed these quarrels and made a real

game out of them. The way things stand, not only the
big organizations such as the Knights of Labor and the
American Federation of Labor found themselves drawing
further and further apart but, in addition, the central
organizations of several big cities and industrial
centers were weakened to the point of powerlessness.
The protocols of the above-mentioned organizations'
sessions made, and make, for very sad reading.

The already frequently mentioned, very conservative
Brotherhood of Locomotive Engineers became involved in a
great struggle with the Ann Arbor railroad at the
beginning of March 1893. The engineers refused to pull
the carriages of this railroad and were therefore placed
under indictment by the federal courts--but in view of
their otherwise exemplary conduct, they received only a
nominal fine, as previously reported. These days a
better spirit seems to pervade this union as well as the
other unions of railway employees. The promising
movement to unify all railway employees and the battles
of the young organization that has grown out of this
conflict, the American Railway Union, will be discussed
in the future in a special section.

The workers, especially the construction workers at
the Worlds Fair in Chicago, fought several skirmishes
during the spring of 1893 with the executive commission
over the eight hour day, and then achieved victory by
the excellent method of over-time which means that they
worked eight hours at their regular daily wage and then
as much overtime as was demanded for higher wages--a
well- known pattern established by various English and
American unions.

The sad state of affairs of the liability
legislation of this country is illustrated by the 47 (or
49) accidents that occurred among these workers,
accidents that were never publicized until
investigations were undertaken. Europeans, especially
Germans and Frenchmen, who came to the Worlds Fair, were
amazed about the lack of security measures that were
taken even during the most dangerous operations.

The American workers received a pleasant surprise
when J. P. Altgeld, the Governor of the State of
Illinois, on June 26th, 1893, pardoned Michael Schwab,
Samuel Fielden and Oskar Neebe, the survivors of the
Anarchist Trial of 1886 who have languished in the state
penitentiary since 1887, and accompanied the pardon with
a sharp and devastating criticism of said trial.
Altgeld himself is a capable jurist, and for many years
he held high judicial offices in Chicago. Therefore his
memorandum which justified the pardon was hardly
attacked by the bourgeois newspapers which limited
themselves to calling Altgeld himself an anarchist. On
the other hand, they made every effort (and it was
successful) during the following autumn to have the
notorious Gary once again occupy the judicial position

that he had disgraced previously.

On the initiative of Altgeld, the legislature of Illinois passed, during the winter of 1892-1893, rather stringent laws for the protection of the female workers, for the limitation of child labor, and for combatting sweat shops and the domestic work of the clothing industry. It was decided to appoint a factory inspectorate in order to enforce these laws. As a chief of this factory inspectorate, Governor Altgeld appointed in July of 1893 Mrs. Florence Kelley, who is well-known to many party comrades in Germany—an appointment which was greeted with great joy. Mrs. Kelley has administered this office until now with discretion and energy, two qualities which are indispensible for the enforcement of these laws in the face of heavy opposition by the exploiters.

The financial crisis has meanwhile during the summer of 1893 hurt the industry badly and hundreds of thousands of workers have been fired or had to put up with serious wage cuts. Already at the end of August 1893, various central bodies of labor leagues or unions turned to state and federal authorities in a plea for protection and help for the unemployed. Either a state of emergency was denied or they were put off with empty promises. Great demands were made upon the treasuries of the unions, the prospects grew and perplexity reigned among the spokesmen for the workers when the British Trade Union Congress gathered at Belfast (Ireland) and came out with the famous resolution about collective property, i.e., the seizure of all of production by society itself. The example proved contagious and soon the most energetic and innovative elements of the labor leagues and unions of the United States gathered new courage and toppled, during the annual convention of the Knights of Labor, Grand Master Workman J. F. Powderly and recommended, during the AFL Convention, an independent political workers' movement which included the following eleven demands:

1. Obligatory schooling
2. Direct legislation
3. Legal eight hour day
4. Health inspection of factories, mines and dwellings
5. Liability of the employers in case of damage to health, body and life
6. Abolition of the system of contracts during all public work
7. Abolition of sweat shops
8. Common ownership of street car, gas and electrical installations for the delivery of light, heat, steam and electrical power for the population
9. Nationalization of telegraphs,

telephones, railways and mines
10. All means of production and distribution
     to be the collective property of the
     people.
11. All legislation to be carried out by a
     referendum.

     The program, which will have to be discussed and
voted upon by all of the affiliated unions, contains the
famous decision of the Belfast Congress under Plank 10.
This step is significant and laudable even though Plank
10 will hardly be accepted on the first try. The
economic development of the country will see to it that
this first step will not remain the only one. And if
this first step really seems difficult, well: c'est
n'est que le premier pas qui coute (it is only the first
step that counts).
     Thus the year 1893 drew to an end with pretty good
prospects for progress of the movement.
     During the winter of 1893-1894, the number of
unemployed workers grew to frightening proportions.
They had to be counted in the hundreds of thousands, and
there were scenes of misery and privation that defied
any description and were not limited to the big cities.
All labor unions and workers' leagues took up the cause
and there occurred a rare phenomenon for New York,
namely the unification of all the different
organizations and sects for a common purpose: to create
help for the unemployed. Unfortunately it did not last.
The attempt was made to get the city authorities moving
and the city officials declared that they were ready to
do all that was in their power but, at the same time,
they admitted their powerlessness under the existing
legal restrictions. A mass meeting was held which went
beautifully but without rendering any help for the
unemployed. A gigantic petition, consisting of at least
50,000 signatures, was to be sent to the legislature.
but that number was never reached, whereupon the whole
movement for the unemployed in New York, which had begun
under such favorable circumstances, crumbled away.
There were riots in Chicago which were put down by the
police's billy clubs. In Boston, thousands of
unemployed marched, under the leadership of a socialist,
in front of and inside of the state house in order to
seek relief from the legislature, and the governor
ordered the police to protect him and the legislators.
Similar events occurred in many other parts of the
country but serious measures to relieve the great
distress were nowhere taken, even though most of the
legislatures were in session at the time. The only
notable exception was provided by the legislature of the
State of New York which empowered the Department of
Public Works of the City of New York to spend the
special sum of one million dollars.[1] The congress, the

national legislature, however, sat in Washington in
comfortable chairs and babbled and babbled about, of all
things, tariffs.

        While these events were occurring for the most
part in the East among the urban and industrial
proletariat in the Midwest and West of the country, a
peculiar movement of small farmers and rural
proletarians, named Coxeyism after its founder Coxey,
prepared itself to undertake no less of a job than, in
the form of a huge army of native unemployed, to move to
Washington, to knock at the gates of congress and to
demand help. This movement has been described before in
the Neue Zeit by others, so I will here merely add that
Coxey's severely diminished group was dispersed by
district and congress police. He himself, as well as a
few other leaders, were arrested and condemned to three
weeks in prison because they all had stepped on the lawn
in front of the Capitol. A short while ago, during the
middle of August, the last remains of this group were
driven by Virginia National Guardsmen into Maryland, and
from there sent into all directions. The President, the
Senate and the House of Representatives had been saved
from the assault and the desires of the poorest who,
after all, are also free and independent citizens of
this land. The federal goverment was saved by the
police, and the bartering of offices and shares of stock
could be resumed without molestation.

        The workers at the coke ovens of Western
Pennsylvania, who are in dire straits and incapable of
prolonging their existence with their starvation wages,
stopped their work last spring and demanded an
improvement of their wages and their situation. They
are a strange mixture of all sorts of nationalities:
Slovaks, Hungarians, Poles, Germans, etc. with Slavs and
Hungarians constituting a majority. The capitalist
papers called them Huns and mocked and jeered at them
because of their poor standard of living. It was,
however, for exactly that reason that they were brought
into this region in droves years ago--because the former
workers were not modest enough but demanded sufficient
wages from the entrepreneurs. Mr. Frick, the
representative of Mr. Carnegie at Homestead and other
places, has many followers here in the coke districts
and he has earned the admiration and respect of the
bourgeoisie, especially Mr. Carnegie. The "Huns," too,
were not at the end of their patience and did not want
to be punished any further; they rebelled against the
hiring of scabs, particularly blacks, that were to take
their place. Under the direction of the highest
judicial officials, the sheriffs and their deputy
sheriffs,[2] a regular hunt began that resembled a hunt
for wild animals. The workers, along with their wives
and children, were driven out of their huts, shot like
deer and left to die in the woods. The crimes that have

been committed by the officials are hair-raising, as the following excerpts from the reports of a bourgeois-Republican newspaper which is published in Pittsburgh illustrates. For better comprehension, be it said that the reporters were in part clergymen who were concerned about their flock. They contacted the German and Austrian envoys so that they could place the workers under protection:

> "At the time we went to Washington, there were about 140 men at the prison in Uniontown of whom many at first had to sleep on the floor. . . . No preparations had been made to feed so many people. An ordinary kitchen stove simply did not suffice. The sheriff himself regretted that the available space was so limited in view of so many prisoners. . . . Could he not have influenced the deputies and sheriffs so they would have proceeded more carefully and more reasonably during their activities (the arrests)? This was hardly contemplated because it was in the interest of the coal and coke barons to break the strike itself by having as many strikers as possible taken into custody. The fact alone that our efforts resulted in a pre-trial hearing after which 70 prisoners had to be released, amply demonstrates the barbaric arbitrariness employed by the so-called deputies in their hunt for innocent people. . . . What do the readers think of the events at Bradford, where the strikers were fired upon as if they were rabid dogs and where a Pole was killed? The next day, after the man had been lying in his blood upon a field for twenty hours, he was loaded on a wagon and buried like a head of cattle. No inquest was held because, supposedly, there were no witnesses. If a mule belonging to one of the operators (employers) had been killed, he certainly would not have been left lying in a field without an "inquest"--but they were dealing only with a Polish coal miner. At Morrell a so-called "organ of public security" stole a watch plus the chain after a man had been led off with his hands tied, and his terrorized wife had fled. Also at Morrell, a horde of bandits, armed with Winchester rifles, dragged an outspoken young German from his home, threw him to the ground, mistreated him then transported him to jail. In Wheeler, the "organs of public security" broke into a house where a young German woman had shortly before given birth to a child. The deputies wanted to arrest her husband who happened to be elsewhere. The woman, who felt relatively well, had fallen asleep with the new-born child in her arms. Suddenly, frightened by the din and

rumble in her room, she perceived a man with a rifle in his hand, standing at her bedside. Who could describe the horror of the new mother? With a loud scream, she falls back upon her pillow and becomes a very ill. . . . The above account offers plenty of material to the unbiased observer to be able to judge the situation of the local coke region. Whoever feels no empathy and sympathy at this point, has no heart for our workers. . . . "

The following sketches concern the blood bath which the bloodthirsty deputy sheriffs carried out on May 24th among the striking coal miners of the same region at Stickle Hollow:

". . . The strikers had succeeded in dissuading those who wanted to go to work from doing so (without threats and without any use of force) when a shot rang out from the ranks of the deputy sheriffs who had been stationed at the workshops. A striker dropped dead, whereupon the bloodthirsty deputies opened up full blast, even though the mass of strikers was fleeing. The shooting was continued as long as the deputies were able to hit anybody. The blood of yesterday's victims of a rapacious company of exploiters cries out to heaven. Just as in Mawood three years ago, the workers in the coal region were shot down by their attackers without warning like dogs yesterday on the public highway before they had attacked any private property. The "representatives of the law" conducted a happy, cheerful and bloodthirsty hunt against the workers who had been pushed together in a bottleneck. . . . While the strikers were withdrawing, they had been driven into a narrow lane where the rifles of those that hunted them were blasting away. In their effort to escape, a detachment of fleeing strikers broke into a wheat field through a barbed-wire fence where, in the end, many of them were captured. Sixty-six strikers were arrested. They were brought back to the coal company, mistreated in the most brutal fashion and locked into box cars which were nailed shut and guarded by 25 murderous deputies. In these box cars, the captives were taken to Uniontown in the evening. The treatment of the captives was similar to the usual infamy shown by their guards and persecutors: the deputies and their landlords."

The above-cited newspaper writes a day later:

"The more details emerge about the blood bath at Stickle Hollow, the more irresponsible, unprovoked and murderous it seems to have been. The property of the Washington Coke and Coal Company, in whose vicinity the shooting of the strikers occurred, is surrounded by high board fences that excluded the possible entry on the part of the strikers. The massacre of the workers was carried out on the open road. Driven by their bad conscience, the owners of the mines ordered a nocturnal inquest by a backwoods justice of the peace from the boondocks of the region who looked at the corpses of the killed workers, brought along willing witnesses to the inquest, and made a judgment which, of course, exonerated the murderous guards of the mining company. Thereupon a storm of protest shook the entire coke and coal region, and the coroner of Uniontown ordered a new post-mortem examination."

A dispatch states as follows:

"All of those shot bore wounds in their backs and thus could not have received their wounds while attacking. Not a single striker was located on the grounds of the coal company; all of them were on the road or on farmland where it was legal for them to be. The Slovak Marlesat was hit by the bullets of his murderous pursuers when he had already covered the distance of half a mile from the coal mine."

Let me give the following excerpts from the already-cited newspaper from Pittsburgh:

"The notorious Lynch, the superintendent of Frick's coke works, recently threw an English family, consisting of a husband, wife and four children (a fifth was soon expected) out into the street with the explanation that a company house was not designed as a maternity home for the wife of a striker. The child was born on the street. Another woman who had observed this inhuman act of expulsion, reopened the door of the house, threw blankets into it and carried the woman back. Whether Frick's coke company will now accuse this woman for breaking and entering remains to be seen. It certainly is possible since anything dastardly may be expected from this company. . . .
"If one observes how in the coke region's vales of misery, law and justice, humaneness and human dignity are trampled upon, then one cannot ignore the fact that the company disregards its obligations. Like the Tsar in Siberia, the coke

baron rules the coke region with absolutist power.
He makes use of the state when it comes to
fulfilling his exploitative desires but, at the
same time, he ignores and mocks laws of the same
state. . . ."
    "A triumph of the coke barons in the present
battle would mean a victory for barbarism and soon
new desperate outbreaks would occur on the part of
the enslaved workers. . . ."
    "The steadfastness of the striking workers of
the coke region is truly magnificent. Even though
flogged out of their huts, replaced by scabs, and
tortured by hunger, they remain firm. The coke
miners who have been mocked so much, seem to have
the courage within them to prefer death rather
than to see themselves degraded to the level of
animals by the dehumanizing slave yoke that the
coke barons want to impose upon them once again.
. . ."

Thus the desperate workers have not given in and
the news persists of new unrest in the coke districts.
Also in the textile industry, which is chiefly
concentrated in the New England states, New Jersey, New
York and Pennsylvania, the workers suffered big wage
reductions and numerous dismissals (because of the lack
of currency as the employers claim) during the summer
and autumn of 1893. In the spring of 1894, therefore,
the silk weavers of Paterson, West Hoboken and New York
began to agitate for the improvement of their situation
which resulted in a stubborn strike at Paterson of a
twelve week duration. It had an unfortunate ending with
a judicial epilogue that has been described previously.
The legislature of Massachusetts issued last winter,
laws for the protection of workers against the
fraudulent practices of factory owners during wage
payments. Furious over this incursion into their
privileges, the factory owners announced several weeks
ago a new wage reduction, and a bitter fight erupted in
the centers of the textile industry at Fall River, New
Bedford and other places. The outcome is not yet
decided.
    The construction and furniture workers have
suffered many a defeat during the past two years which
could not be avoided given the existing rate of
unemployment, even though these workers are well-
organized. Similar news must be reported from the
numerous workers in the leather, shoe and boot industry.
The once flourishing jewelry industry has been doing
badly for years. Its workers are employed for only
three to four months and at miserable wages. The
tailors are beset by the cottage industry and the sweat
shops which produce the same serious evils as exist
elsewhere. Important branches of the clothing industry,

as for example, the manufacture of caps, hoods, and
ladies coats are completely (and other branches, for the
main part) in the hands of Jewish workers who earn very
low wages. A few years ago, these workers founded a
respectable Jewish labor union and in New York they have
even formed a central body of this union. Big strikes
are presently an everyday occurrence and the prospects
are good for the workers even though they feud with each
other.

The iron and steel industry has receded greatly,
and with it the great association of the United Iron and
Steel Workers. Just how significant the general
recession of this industry has been is illustrated by
the following news that has been verified: one of the
largest machine factories of the country that, until the
late summer of 1893, employed over 1400 workers has
reduced its work force to hardly five hundred.

It is the same everywhere: in the cities, in the
countryside, in the east, in the west and in the south.

It is understandable that under these
circumstances, the miners, particularly those employed
in coal production, had to suffer. Their wages had
dropped so low that a desperate battle seemed
inevitable. In spite of the unfavorable circumstances,
the organization of the miners (particularly the
centralization of the individual branches) has made
significant progress. At the beginning of April of this
year, a conference of miners' delegates was held at
Columbus, Ohio, and it was unanimously decided to demand
better wages and working conditions for the miners and
to back up these demands by a general strike if it
should become necessary. The demands of the workers
were rejected and on April 21st a strike began all along
the line (except for the anthracite districts of
Pennsylvania) in the states of Pennsylvania, Ohio,
Indiana, Illinois, West Virginia, Kentucky, Tennessee,
Iowa, Missouri, Kansas, Colorado, and Alabama. The
fight was rough. The employers attempted to fill the
positions of the strikers by scabs especially in
Alabama, West Virginia, Illinois, and Colorado, and they
threw the old workers, who for the most part lived in
company houses, out of their homes and cut off their
credit at the company store. Thereupon the miners,
supported by their brave wives, got together, drove away
the scabs, allowed no train filled with scabs to stop,
and chased away the company officials. Particularly
serious incidents occurred in Alabama where the
employers wanted to hire blacks; in Illinois where
Governor Altgeld, after much hesitation and with great
reluctance, called up the National Guard; in Western
Pennsylvania; in Kansas; and in Colorado. A description
of the fight in Western Pennsylvania by the coke workers
has been rendered previously.

The struggle between the miners and the mine owners
at Cripple Creek, Colorado, took on peculiar forms since
a struggle over jurisdiction broke out between the
bourgeois authorities. The miners after occupying the
mines had entrenched themselves so that the mine owners
could not even enter their property, much less install
scabs there. The owners, therefore, asked the county
sheriff to remove the miners. The sheriff, a good
bourgeois who believed in exploitation, knew full well
that in the mines he was facing courageous people so he
swore in as his deputy sheriffs a large group of
cutthroat idlers before he commenced his attack which
was initially repelled by the miners. While the sheriff
now swore in even more predatory riff-raff, the
beleaguered miners turned to the governor of the state,
a so-called populist, i.e., a member of the People's
Party (the party of the small farmers) and asked him to
intervene in their favor by appointing a mediation
board. The governor agreed and asked the sheriff to
withdraw his forces. When the sheriff refused to do so,
the governor called up the National Guard to rout the
sheriff. There were skirmishes, and a regular battle
between the National Guard and the sheriff's forces
seemed imminent when a last-minute truce was arranged
which was based on the withdrawal of the deputy
sheriffs. These people, as well as other adherents and
officials of the mine owners, were so incensed over the
humiliation they had suffered that they kidnapped the
assistant of the governor and tarred and feathered him
as a punishment for taking the side of the workers. A
typical bourgeois act, wasn't it? In Tennessee,
approximately the same scenes recurred as two years ago
because once again the attempt was made to use convicts
from penitentiaries as scabs against the strikers.
There was heavy action everywhere because most of the
miners had lost their patience and had acted roughly at
times. When a few heads were bashed in and a few
barracks were burnt down and the bourgeois press began
to sob, the leaders, i.e., the officials of the miners
national association led by President John McBride,
became weak, wrapped themselves in the mantle of
respectability, dissociated themselves from the acts of
violence and wanted to end the strike officially. This
however, only succeeded part way by mid-June. In many
places, the strikes are still being continued by the
miners and they are holding the bourgeois authorities at
bay.
      As may be gathered from the preceding account,
there was much action during the first six months of
1894. Everywhere, the workers fought against the
consequences of the present crisis and defended
themselves energetically against the efforts of the
bourgeois employers to push the standard of living of
the proletarians even lower. The bourgeoisie had not

yet digested the Coxeyites, coke workers and miners,
when the ground under their feet began to shake once
again from the march of new battalions and the American
Railway Union entered upon the stage.

Chapter VI: Endnotes

[1] Only recently, on September 2nd, 1894, the Comptroller of New York City reported that about half of this amount had been spent and it is reported (and can hardly be doubted) that the money was spent for political purposes.

[2] A sheriff has the right to hire (swear in) deputy sheriffs to aid him. He can hire as many as he wants to and these days deputy sheriffs are usually the most unscrupulous scum of the whole region, resembling the Pinkerton people who have been described earlier. No decent person would want to join them. At Hammond, Indiana, the sheriff recently could not find a single citizen who wanted to be sworn in as a deputy sheriff.

7

The American Railway Union and the Pullman Strike

In earlier accounts, there was much mention of the numerous organizations of railroad employees and workers of this country: the engineers, the firemen, the brakemen, the conductors, the switchmen, etc. There was mention of the attempts to fuse all of these individual unions or to have them join with one of the large labor unions such as the Knights of Labor or the American Federation of Labor, of the obstacles which this hoped-for concentration of forces encountered, of the persons who hindered this progress, etc. I have reported earlier about the strike of the switchmen at Buffalo and the miners at Tennessee, and I cited parts of an article by E. V. Debs (the president of the American Railway Union who has been mentioned frequently as of late) that deals with this matter from which I would like to quote once again the following sentence: "The unification of all railway employees in one body is the task of my life."

Debs at that time resigned his position as highest official of the Brotherhood of Locomotive Firemen in order to work with the pen as editor of the organ of the firemen and as organizer and founder of a new organization that would unite all workers and employees of the railways and related unions without dissolving the existing unions of the individual railway-related jobs. Older labor union leaders regarded the undertaking as risky and premature, but Debs would not let himself be deterred. The conditions, which became more and more intolerable, prepared the soil for him and energetic colleagues, who were dissatisfied with the heretofore existing fragmentation, joined him so that his undertaking registered amazing progress and achieved many successes. Whereas the old unions, which had remained untouched, chiefly served supportive purposes, the new organization was designed from the very start for offensive purposes: to achieve better working conditions, to achieve full solidarity among all railroad workers, and to cease making distinctions between engineers, switchmen, conductors, firemen, etc. They were all subjected to the same exploitation by the same persons or companies, and they had thus the same interests for which they were called upon to fight as brothers.

During the strike at the Reading Railway a few years ago, the members of the Brotherhood of Locomotive Engineers replaced the striking Knights of Labor . Not long afterward, the Knights of Labor hurried to the West in order to repay the "Brotherhood" tit for tat.   During the great strike at Buffalo in August 1892, the switchmen were left miserably in the lurch.   During the Ann Arbor strike (1893) it was the turn of the engineers, etc.   Such events made people think and made them receptive to the propaganda for a new, all-encompassing organization which called itself the American Railway Union.

The great expanse of the railway system of the United States is well known.   What is not generally known is the fact that the American railway companies exploit their workers and employees more by far and that they damage their lives more extensively than any other railway does in the world.   According to an official report, the English railways employed on the average 1,748 persons per 100 English miles; the American railways, however, only 459.   In England 1 out of 875 persons was killed; in the United States 1 out of 459 railway workers lost his life.   In England 1 out of 158 men was injured; in the United States, 1 out of 35.   The degree of exploitation and the lack of consideration in the United States is truly astonishing.   How much they enjoyed curtailing the wages of their employees was illustrated by the railway administrations during the summer of 1893.   At the first sign of the financial crisis, and at a time when they were still enjoying higher revenues because of the world fair traffic they cut the wages immediately and formed an alliance for the purpose of systematically reducing wages.

Increased exploitation, ruthless treatment, steadily growing dangers at work, reduced wages and long working hours--these are certainly reasons for dissatisfaction and the necessary fuel for an explosion.

In faithful observation of the principle of the new organization to pull together all branches of the railway service and its related unions into one great body, the workers (about 4,000) employed at the Pullman Palace and Sleeping Car Company at the town of Pullman, a suburb of Chicago, were taken into the American Railway Union.   Mr. George M. Pullman had built this town in connection with his railway carriage factory

with apartment buildings for "his" workers, with
schools, churches, stores, etc., and thousands of
workers moved there in order to receive spiritual and
material food, housing, fire and light from him.
Everything is delivered and sold for hefty and assured
prices which Mr. Pullman usually deducts, without any
discussion, directly from the wages which his people
receive in his factory, the only place of work in town.
Mr. Pullman, who had himself extravagantly praised and
eulogized for all of the beautiful contrivances which he
had created for the welfare of his workers, happens to
have become a very, very rich man, a multi-millionaire
on the side (or because of all these institutions). In
the end, following a well-known custom, he transformed
his business into a corporation at the top of which he
stands as president while the administration is handed
down to other officials. Nobody has any right to
interfere with the administration of the town of
Pullman, which is run by Mr. Pullman himself, but
unfortunately he has not been able to take away the
voting rights of the town, the state and the entire
country. In the autumn of 1892 his workers caused him
great grief when they voted overwhelmingly for the
Democratic candidates Altgeld and Cleveland, whereas Mr.
Pullman is an ardent adherent of the Republican Party
and a warm admirer of former President Harrison. Mr.
Harrison had shortly before the election appointed Mr.
Pullman's special friend, Mr. Grosscup, as federal judge
for Chicago. Mr. Pullman was deeply hurt by the
insubordination of his workers and made use of the first
opportunity to show his displeasure by cutting their
wages while insisting on receiving the same prices for
his delivery contracts, as a minister in the Pullman
community openly and uncontestedly revealed. These wage
cuts were sporadically continued until the situation of
the workers became well-nigh unbearable. Earlier this
year, the workers owed $80,000 in rent alone without the
slightest prospect of being able to pay this debt.
While the exterior appearance of the houses, streets and
squares was kept scrupulously clean, misery reigned
sometimes in the interior where numerous families
frequently lived in a single room in order to survive.
The father of a young girl, who had worked fifteen years
for the Pullman Company, died in shabby surroundings
while still owing the company $60 for rent. The unpaid
bill was sent to his orphaned daughter who had to pay
the bill bit by bit from her 30 cents a day and from her
brother's wages of 70 cents a day. Several days before
the strike, a worker received a paycheck which was 45
cents less than his rent which was due, etc.
     During February of this year, a general reduction
of wages between 25 and 33 1/3 % and even up to 50% was
announced. The workers then held a meeting (nobody knew
who had organized it because nobody dared to do such a

thing openly at Pullman). The workers sent a delegation
to Mr. Pullman in order to tell him that the workers
could not exist with such wages and in order to ask him
to reduce at least the rents along with the wages.
Instead of considering the rents, the delegation was
summarily dismissed and its members were quickly fired
from their jobs. On May 7th the workers at Pullman
stopped work and thus began the strike at Pullman.
      Mr. Pullman claimed that he could not enter into
negotiations with his employees because the Pullman
Company was working at a loss. The falsehood of this
assertion clearly emerges from an official declaration
which the company made two months before the strike and
where one can read verbatim: "The day is near when the
present 30 million capital will be covered and more than
covered by the value of the 3500 acres of land upon
which the town of Pullman has been built." At the same
time, it was announced that the 30 million capital stock
has a market value of 60 million dollars.
      The strike (at Pullman, be it remembered) broke out
because the workers could not live from their reduced
wages. An aid society was formed in order to help these
people and to provide them with food, and it is claimed
that these people lived better from these hardly
adequate supplies than they had previously from the
wages which Mr. Pullman had paid them. The aid
committee for the Pullman strikers visited a number of
organizations, among them the first annual convention of
the American Railway Union which met during the third
week in June at Chicago, and asked for moral and
financial support. The convention sent a delegation to
the Pullman Company and asked it to resolve the conflict
through a mediation board, but the Pullman Company
stated that there was nothing to arbitrate and that it
was refusing to even discuss the matter. Having been
both insulted and hurt in this manner, the convention
decided with great enthusiasm to declare a boycott of
the Pullman Company, to refuse to do any work for the
company, and to call upon all workers to do likewise if
the Pullman Company would not come to an agreement with
its workers or submit its conflict to compulsory
arbitration. The company was given a grace period of
three days. The company ignored the convention and
placed the matter before the railway administrations and
the executive of the General Managers' Association which
had already been founded in 1893 in order to plan common
action against the workers. It was decided that the
Pullman affair was to be regarded and treated as its own
business.
      On June 26th the members of the American Railway
Union set to work with admirable order and discipline,
and within a few days the entire railway traffic of
Chicago was paralyzed along with the gigantic industries
that are concentrated in Chicago which provide the

country with meat, agricultural and mining machinery, etc. Similar events occurred in Cincinnati, Cleveland, Omaha, San Francisco and many other cities of the Midwestern and Western states. A few railway administrators even interrupted the traffic with Pullman and, after the passage of four to five days, it seemed that one could congratulate the American Railway Union for a complete victory when suddenly the federal courts intervened and issued injunctions against Debs and his colleagues under the pretext of having obstructed the mail by the violent actions of the strikers. Pullman's friend (see above), Judge Grosscup, issued the first injunction on July 2nd, and the other federal judges followed his example wherever the opportunity existed. The strikers were not at all opposed to the dispatch of mail, but they demanded that no Pullman carriages be attached to mail trains. The train company officials, however, defiantly attached Pullman cars to the mail trains and there occurred, just as the train executives had hoped for, interruptions in the delivery of the mail. The postmaster of Chicago, in conjunction with other federal officials, asked President Cleveland for military protection of the mail delivery, and the President immediately responded to the request and allowed federal troops to move into Chicago.

On July 5th the Governor of the State of Illinois, the already often-mentioned J. P. Altgeld, protested immediately and vehemently against the entry of federal troops and declared that the state was perfectly able and ready to maintain order within its borders. He described the intervention of the United States military forces as a maneuver of the General Managers' Association to obtain people for the train service. He said: "At the moment, there are some railroads that are paralyzed, but not by obstructions (on the part of the strikers) but because they have no crews. They would like to keep all of this secret. That is why they scream about 'obstructions.' They want to divert people's attention from the truth." The governor cites two specific cases as examples and concludes: "To ignore completely a local (state) government in matters of this kind when that same government is ready to lend all necessary help in the carrying out of the laws of the United States is not only an insult against the people of that state but also a violation of the basic principles of our institutions." The President refuted none of the governor's arguments but in his reply referred to his legal authority and the call for his intervention on the part of federal offices and officials. Altgeld replied sharply that the interpretation of the law by the President was of a dubious nature, that the federal officials were subjects and creatures of the President, whose appeals to the President gave him power equal to that of the Russian

Tsar,and he demanded the immediate withdrawal of the
federal troops. On July 6th Cleveland gave this
hypocritical and lachrymose reply:

> Whereas I am still convinced not to have exceeded
> my authority and duty,it seems to me that in this
> hour of danger and public emergency,discussion
> must give way to strong efforts on the part of all
> those in authority to have the law respected and
> life and property respected."

On the next day,the president released a
proclamation to all of the good citizens of the City of
Chicago to remain calm and to stay in their houses,a
proclamation which was tantamount to a declaration of a
state of siege. One day later the same proclamation was
issued for the states of North Dakota,Montana,Idaho,
Wyoming,Washington,Colorado and California and to the
territories of New Mexico and Utah--all of which
illustrates the extent and significance of the movement.
Chicago resembled an armed camp,and during the
first few days after the entry of the federal troops,a
conflict threatened to break out between them and the
National Guard,a conflict which the urban mob wanted.
The regular troops were received in a very cold and
reluctant manner,and they soon made use of their
weapons according to their instructions on July 9th
which had been kept secret for some time: You (the
soldiers) do not have to care how great the casualties
may be among the public enemies (sic!). Just make your
blows count so that all resistance will promptly be
crushed." In Hammond,a little town along the border
between Illinois and Indiana,the officials sent to
investigate the situation did not find any reason to
intervene,and the sheriff did not find a single citizen
who was willing to serve as an auxiliary sheriff. It
was perhaps exactly for this reason that the US.
military was sent to create a blood bath among the
peaceful spectators. In Chicago,the sheriff and
federal marshal (the latter has the same function in
federal matters as the sheriff has in state affairs)
swore in a great number of auxiliary sheriffs and
marshals,and these deputies",who were the dregs of
society,were the real rioters and disturbers of the
peace--which was proven later by an investigation that
agreed with the accounts of newspaper reporters and the
city police. The greatest disturbances occurred in
California at Sacramento,Oakland,Los Angeles and other
towns. In California there exists almost universal
bitterness towards the large corrupt and corrupting
Pacific railroads. The strikers there would not let
themselves be cowed by the proclamation of the president
or by the intervention of the regular federal troops.
The population sympathized with the strikers,and the

U.S. military had a tough time and even suffered some
casualties. In all of the already named states and
territories and in many others, as for example, in Ohio,
Michigan, Wisconsin, Minnesota, etc., etc., there were
disturbances and unrest; everywhere the federal courts
intervened and, for the most part, the federal troops
too.
      During these events, and as a consequence of them,
there occurred a great shortage of meat in the populated
East because no animals were going toward Chicago and no
meat was coming from there, and the bourgeois papers
were lamenting the lack of meat. As mentioned before,
the Attorney-General ordered the federal attorney at
Chicago to appoint a special grand jury. Its members
were gathered from the most remote corners of the
district, and they were most willing to raise
accusations against the officials and members of the
American Railway Union. Debs and others were arrested
and released only after paying a huge bail ($10,000).
Shortly thereafter, they were arrested once more because
of their alleged defiance of a judicial injunction. Debs
and his comrades refused to pay bail once again, and
they let themselves be jailed at the Cook County Jail
which had become famous as a result of the anarchist
trial. The Mayor of Chicago, accompanied by prominent
citizens of the city and members of the American Railway
Union, turned directly to the Pullman Company with the
request to put an end to the unrest by appointing a
board of mediation. Mr. Pullman himself has long taken
off for the East to his villa on the Thousand Islands in
the St. Lawrence River after emptying his palace of all
objects of value and after placing it under the special
control of the police and the national guard. His right
hand man, however, the Second Vice President, Wickes,
told the mayor coldly: "There is nothing to arbitrate,"
and the mayor had to put up with this insult just as the
workers and their representatives had to at an earlier
time.
      The new Grand Master of the Knights of Labor called
upon the Knights of Labor to help and to strike without
meeting with much of a response. The Executive Board of
the AFL was called to Chicago in order to undertake
measures in support of the strikers, but it refused to
organize a sympathy strike; it merely released a
declaration of support for the strikers, a sort of
petition to President Cleveland and an appeal to collect
money for Debs and his comrades.
      It was too late; the workers were conquered and
suppressed by federal soldiers and federal courts, and
on July 16th the House of Representatives at Washington,
Republicans as well as Democrats, without division (that
is, an exact vote count was not made out of cowardice)
expressed its approval of the actions of the President
and his cabinet. Only two members of congress--a

Populist and a Democrat--expressed some concern. The strike was given up if not directly called off.

The federal government had felt uneasy about the tremendous display of force which was used to suppress the workers who, after all, also vote; all the more so as these workers could not be labeled aliens or anarchists. When, therefore, the trial against Debs, because of contempt of court, was scheduled for July 25th, the federal attorney under all sorts of invalid pretexts asked for an adjournment of the trial until September. The obliging judge immediately granted this request, but not before the attorney for the defense had told him a few cutting things to his face about the whole nature of these proceedings. Time was thus gained, and the excitement in the entire country, as well as the displeasure shown even in certain bourgeois circles over the injunction fraud, will probably have died down somewhat.

On August 2nd, the Pullman Company reopened its factory with about 250 (mostly new) people. Four thousand workers are unemployed because the company employs no one that participated in the strike, and great suffering reigns among them, which is augmented by the fact that the company obtained court orders to expel the workers from their dwelling places. Governor Altgeld inspected the town of Pullman personally and discovered much misery and distress. He attempted to persuade Pullman to help but to no avail. He then appealed for help to the entire state on August 22nd. Pullman's black list was displayed during the questioning of the investigation committee. The black list of the railroad administrators functions in all parts of the country that are dominated by the General Managers' Association, and Egan, the chairman of the latter, has admitted as much. Fillmore, the general superintendent of the South Pacific Railroad, told a reporter in San Francisco the following:

> "If I know a man who has not remained loyal to his railroad and I find out that he has found work elsewhere, I will persecute him until I have succeeded in his dismissal. These guys who ruined our locomotives, destroyed our property, and killed our employees(?) shall never earn their bread in California if I can help it. . . . I do not need characters of this kind, and as far as my arm can reach they are not going to find any bread."

Let me relate a few but characteristic episodes of the Pullman Strike.

A federal judge in Topeka (Kansas) prohibited the striking railway workers of a certain union at Argentine (Kansas) from damaging the property of the railroad or

proceeding in any other way against the railway. At the
same time he ordered them to appear personally before
the court of Topeka on August 6th. Four hundred members
of this union met on August 1st to talk over the matter
and authorized their secretary to send the following
letter to Judge Scarrett in Topeka:

> Dear Sir:
>   Speaking for myself as well as in the name of
> the other people of this town who have received a
> court summons for the first week in August, permit
> me to say that we are not aware of having violated
> any law whatsoever and we see, therefore, no
> justification for spending money for a railway
> trip to appear before you, and we will also not
> hire a lawyer for our defense. If other court
> summons are sent with as little justification as
> in our case, then our boasted justice and freedom
> are no more permanent than the handle of an
> earthen jar and we will not try any resistance.
> You may find us in Argentine, as soon as you want
> to get hold of us.
>
> Sincerely,
G. S. McFadden,
Secretary

What the judge did thereupon was not reported.
    The esteem in which the scabs are held here is
illustrated by the following scene that occurred on
August 6th at Pullman, which had been occupied by the
National Guard.
    At 1:30 p.m. Company M under the command of
Sergeant Cook marched to the entrance of the mess tent.
Inside the tent they saw tables occupied by scabs from
the Pullman Company who had been placed next to the
guardsmen because they were afraid to go home to eat.
William Byrnes, a National Guard soldier, stepped
through the tent entrance and said: "The members of
Company M are here as voluntary soldiers to see to it
that the laws of the State of Illinois are respected. I
cannot imagine that the honor of a soldier of our
discipline would force us to do something that we
consider unpatriotic and unworthy of a gentleman. My
principles command me not to communicate with scabs. I
refuse to sit at the same table with them." Byrne's
comrades applauded enthusiastically, and a dozen voices
exclaimed: "We are not entering the tent as long as the
scabs are inside." The scabs were finally let out and
the National Guard company marched into the tent having
obtained the promise that from now on they could use the
mess tent for themselves.

Chapter VII: Endnotes

[1]The American Federationist (Samuel Gompers)
informs us that this Grosscup said in a speech of May
30th: "The growth of labor organizations must be
checked by law." Mr. Grosscup later modified this
quotation and declared that he had actually said: "Let
us set a limit to the field of organization." As one
can see: the meaning remains the same.

8
The Investigation Committee—Postscript

The Knights of Labor sent a delegation to President Cleveland with the request that he establish, on the basis of a former law, a commission of arbitration to investigate the Pullman Strike. The AFL even demanded that the President himself come to Chicago in order to see what was going on. President Cleveland has better things to do. He attends, rather, hunting parties in North Carolina or he goes fishing in the great bays of the Atlantic coast. Transportation and food there are supplied by the government. If neither hunting nor fishing are on the agenda, he retires to his ostentatious country retreat in Massachusetts. To Chicago he dispatches his generals and corporals, his judges and similar riffraff. He did, however, do the Knights of Labor a favor and appointed an investigation commission of three persons headed by the labor and census statistician C. D. Wright.

The committee met during the second week in August at Chicago in order to collect testimonies for its report. Of these testimonies, the most important ones, those of Debs, Pullman and Wickes, will be related in excerpt form. At first, the gentlemen usually gave a general description of the strike (naturally from their point of view and class interest), and then followed the questions of the committee members and the corresponding answers.

Debs testified as follows:

"I received the news of an eminent strike at Pullman and I went to Chicago to investigate the matter. I found out that the people at the Pullman Company have to work for wages that do not allow them to exist properly. I found that the wages were cut again and again up to a point where

even skilled and learned workers had to slave away
for wages that would have been insufficient for an
ordinary day laborer. I found that the town of
Pullman with its factories, houses and stores, was
so arranged that every cent earned by the workers
wandered back into the coffers of the company. I
found that in reality the workers at Pullman were
in a pitiable condition, and I decided that in my
capacity as president of the American Railway
Union I would do everything possible to improve
their condition. The strike occurred (at Pullman)
and the workers themselves declared it. Then
followed the boycott (of the Pullman cars) which
was declared by legally elected delegates of our
convention, and then followed the strikes against
the railroad companies which were decided upon and
declared by the different union locals, each one
having its own complaints. . . . "

Debs then related the course of the strike, and
Commissioner Wright asked him whether the railroad
strikes would have taken place without the difficulties
with Pullman. Debs answered:

"No! The Pullman strike (in the spring) was
the main cause. We wanted to paralyze the Pullman
cars and curtail the revenues in order to force
the company to submit the conflict to arbitration.
But the railroad companies, too, had their own
complaints and accusations. The General Managers'
Association had been founded with the openly
expressed intention to assist the individual
railroad company that was experiencing labor
trouble. Its obvious aim was the destruction of
the labor organizations. The association had
hardly been founded when a systematic reduction of
wages at all of the railroads of the country
occurred. The reductions occurred first at one
railroad and in one department alone, but the
regularity with which they occurred was very
significant! The people (the workers) wanted to
stop their work and they felt justified in doing
so. But without this Pullman business, nothing
would have happened. Times were unfavorable:
there was a slump in business, and money was
scarce. I did not order the strike. I had no
power to do so; the people did it themselves.
This does not mean that I want to shirk
responsibility. I say gladly that I agreed with
it entirely and that I approved the actions of
these people. I have always condemned acts of
violence and I have written and spoken against
them. . . . "

Debs then stated that the American Railway Union had defeated the railway companies within five days of the declaration of the strike (boycott):

"They were paralyzed, but it so happened that just around this time it was raining injunctions, and shortly thereafter the officials of the American Railway Union were arrested for contempt of court. That is what beat us. Not the railroad companies, and not the army, but the power of the United States courts conquered us. General Miles, the commanding general of the troops who had been sent to Chicago, came to Chicago, looked up the General Managers' Association, and stated in an interview the following day that he had broken the back of the strike. He had as little right to confer with the General Managers' Association as he would have had to consult with the people of our union. I would also like to say that it appears very strange that all of our letters and dispatches have been declared public property (by publication) whereas not a single line of the train company officials' correspondence has been published. If this correspondence had been published too, I could prove that the railway company directors declared in one of their secret sessions that they would stamp the American Railway Union out of existence."

Mr. George M. Pullman, the founder and president of the Pullman Company, testified as follows:

"The Pullman Company was founded in 1867 with a capital of one million dollars. The present capital amounts to 36 million dollars. The company has paid dividends since it existed. For three years it paid 3% every quarter. One year it paid 9 1/2% annually; later, an annual 8% was paid."

Asked whether the Pullman Company had made a profit of 16 million dollars, Mr. Pullman answered:

"The profit was greater."
Question: "Has the company made or lost money during this past year?"
Answer: "It has earned money. It paid the usual 8% dividends which came to about 2,800,000 dollars."

About the founding of the town of Pullman during the year 1880, he said the following:

"The plan was to found a settlement where the
workers would live in harmony with the company.
The relations between the company and its people
remained, however, that of a landlord and his
tenants. The profit from the rents must be
estimated at 6% but, of course, the costs
connected with the layout of the streets, etc.,
must not be disregarded. Real estate was not sold
in this town because the company wanted to make
sure it controlled the inhabitants."

Question: "Do the same people that control the
Pullman Car Company also control the Pullman Land
Company?"
Answer: "There is no control. The car company
possesses all shares of the land company so that, in
fact, there is only one company. The average increase
of the car company's capital growth amounted to about a
million a year. Once the increase was six million. The
capital profits amounted to 25 million. As far as the
wage reductions are concerned, I have to refer you to
persons that were specifically concerned with that. I
do not remember that the Pullman Company ever tried to
solve the difficulties by a court of arbitration. I am
personally opposed to any court of arbitration."
Question: "Do you not think, Mr. Pullman, that a
company such as yours, which made so much money during
the last few years that it was able to pay out 2,800,000
dollars in dividends, could give a part of these profits
to the workers (at Pullman)?"
Answer: "The factory department at Pullman is
totally separate from the other departments of the
company. The factory department has worked at a loss and
I do not see why on earth there should be an increase in
wages in a department that has lost money just because
the company as a whole has made a profit."
Question: "Has the company ever raised the wages
during those years when it registered extraordinary
profits?"
Answer: "No!"
Question: "Would it not have been fair to give to
the workers at least enough so that they could lead a
reasonable existence?"
Answer: "I do not believe that. That would have
been a gift of money to the workers. One has to view
this whole matter instead from the viewpoint of
business. The company had to make sacrifices, and the
workers were expected to do the same."
Mr. Pullman professed to know very little about the
leases with their oppressive clauses and the money for
these leases, as well as the rent itself which was
deducted from workers' wages.
Question: "Were the rents lowered when the wages
were reduced?"

Answer: "No."
Question: "Were the wages of yourself and other
executives reduced?"
Answer: "No."
Question: "Why not?"
Answer: "If we would reduce the wages of the
executives, they would leave our company."
Mr. Wickes, Second Vice-President and Executive of
the Pullman Company, stated:

> "The profit (of the company) amounts to
> between 2 and 10%. The demand for higher wages
> cannot be met on principle in order to prevent
> further demands at a later time."

Question: "Has the Pullman Company ever increased
their wages voluntarily?"
Answer: "In a few individual cases, but not in
general."
Question: "Would it not be better to raise wages
during good times or, in other words, to adjust the
wages according to the level of the profits?"
Answer: "No. This would only lead to confusion.
We obtain workers on the free market place just as we
buy materials. We act according to the law of supply
and demand."
Question: "Can the question of wages not be
resolved by a court of arbitration?"
Answer: "No, the company alone knows what wages it
should pay."
Question: "What is your attitude towards the
unions?"
Answer: "We negotiate with our people as
individuals and not as members of a union."
Question: "Do you believe these people can really
assert themselves against the company as individuals?"
Answer: "If they cannot speak for themselves, that
is their business."
Question: "You do not believe that the workers
have the right to organize themselves in order to do
away with wrongs?
Answer: "No. If they do not like to work for the
wages that we have set, they have the privilege to go
elsewhere."
This language is clear and of laudable frankness.
The petty bourgeois is indeed crying and weeping
over the fact that Mr. Pullman did not pull any of his
punches and that he asserted and maintained his right to
exploit people without any embarrassment. They thunder
against his eviction order; they call Pullman "a
gruesome employer," "a traitor to his own obligations
towards the community" etc. During the strike, however,
this sad crew could only heap calumny and hatred upon
the workers. The exploiters themselves, whether singly,

in associations, or in their newspapers, recognize full
well the significance of such events as the Pullman
strike, and they are ready to stop it from spreading by
all available means. Thus, for example, the editor of
the chief organ of the iron industry, the Iron Age,
writes:

>   " . . . Let us face it: This strike was no
> explosion of certain employees against certain
> companies, but rather a demonstration in favor of
> all organized labor against the employers. It was
> an insurrection of certain parts of the wage
> earners' class against the existing society. . . .
> Former disorders were only sporadic eruptions. . .
> .This most recent strike exposes a deeply rooted
> disease--a cancerous growth--which cannot be
> extirpated without insuring the adjacent tissue
> and without bloodshed; its existence threatens the
> nation."

Whereas the American bourgeoisie and its press are
distinguished in general by their cynicism and
brutality, and cover their naked statues with fig leaves
(but not their naked self-interest), there were and
there are also parts of them that cloak themselves with
pious ways of thinking and feign a certain
respectability so that they may pander to their lust for
profits without being observed. Sometimes because of
stupidity, sometimes out of strict calculations, these
sorts of people hide their heads in the sand. After the
big unemployment movement of last winter, after the
strikes in the coke region, after Coxey's March on
Washington, and after the coal miners' strike with its
bloodshed and its disturbances--the main organ of the
Manchester people of the United States New York Evening
Post begged for hushing up:

>   "The way the world is today, we believe that
> it is the highest duty of all writers, preachers
> and professors who are active in the reform
> movement, to refrain from all attacks upon the
> existing society and the existing societal
> institutions. . . . "

Then came the Pullman strike and, after it was
crushed, the same newspaper was enchanted by the
appearances and testimonies of Mssrs. Pullman and Wickes
and wrote:

>   "Mr. Pullman took a firm position, as a
> matter of fact the only possible position, by
> facing foursquare all the anarchistic views which
> lurked in the questions that he was being asked.
> Instead of trying to assuage, to apologize and to
> ameliorate, he grabbed the bull by its horns."

The intervention of the federal authorities
and their open partisanship for the bourgeois
exploiters has simplified the situation in the
United States considerably. The so-called states'
rights, against which the workers have often
smashed their heads, have been violated in many
ways by the recent events and thus a gap has been
opened through which the workers can occasionally
break through. Of great significance was the
lesson that the workers were taught, namely that
Democrats and Republicans (in the American sense
of the words) are only different names for the
bourgeois exploiting parties--a lesson which can
only be of help to the labor movement of this
country.

The small peasant party of the so-called
Populists tried to take advantage of this
situation. It did not only offer sympathy to the
strikers, but it often offered and gave real aid.
After all, the workers were battling the big
railraod companies which had long been attacked
and threatened by the Populists. Many labor
organizations are entering into alliances with the
Populists that are similar to the one entered upon
a number of years ago by the Knights of Labor and
the Populists. Even "socialists" in the various
cities of the West are making common cause with
the Populists, and it may be assumed that the
latter's gains in the elections this fall will not
be insignificant. If the workers during this
year, as is to be hoped, have often been rudely
emancipated from the Republicans and the
Democrats, they will be at a later time (probably
in a similar fashion) cured of their sympathies
for the Populists.

It remains to be seen what the big labor
unions of the country will do at their conventions
later this year. The order of the Knights of
Labor has cruised until now almost exclusively in
the small farmer and petit-bourgeois channels, and
it allowed itself to be taken in tow by the silver
hobgoblins and the Populists. It is hardly to be
expected that the Knights of Labor will now become
more independent since the order has lost
influence because of the drop in membership.

The locals of the AFL, as has been mentioned
earlier, are discussing the program (initiated in
1893) of an independent policy with the
collectivist Plank 10 which has not met with much
support until now. The obsequiousness which the
AFL displayed during the strike of the American
Railway Union has been widely resented in many
places and organizations, and it is expected that
it will probably act more energetically in the
future.

The ferment in the various organizations of the railroad workers and employees continues,of course,strongly. It cannot be predicted, however,whether the American Railway Union will profit from this and overcome its defeat,because one has to take into account the idiosyncracies of the country and the human material.

In spite of the gigantic economic development,in spite of the amazing growth of industry,in spite of the capitalistic exploitation which is stifling everything,the labor movement in the United States is still,in a certain sense,in an infantile stage. It jumps here and there but,until now,it has not jumped into the socialist camp from which it is protected (to use a variation of Schäffles well-known expression) by the anti-collectivist skull of the American worker.

It is true that there exists a socialist movement in this country but,whenever it surfaces,it is of a German variety,and it also appears predominantly in the German language. As much as this movement might at times be useful as far as its theoretical propaganda and schooling is concerned,it has very little influence upon the often throbbing lives and organizations of the workers.

Socialist ideology has not yet penetrated the popular masses,even though they have enough socialist thoughts within them,ie,the urge to transform the conditions of society to a more just state and in a way that will appeal to the broad masses. It cannot come as a surprise that in such a young country the nationalization of the railroads and telegraphs is described as a socialist demand.

The big industry of this country is still being hindered by custom barriers,and its very important power of expansion is limited by import taxes on raw materials. Once the beginning is made to remove them,American industry will enter the world market and the American workers,once they find themselves in competition with the European proletarians,will also get rid of their traditional whims. England,whose labor movement has always exercised great influence upon the American one,will continue the course that it has pursued for a number of years and will certainly influence the United States.

A European party comrade,who is intimately acquainted with the above-mentioned conditions, gave to one of his American friends the following opinions concerning the last-mentioned points:

"Your life is filled with great ups and downs
. . . but every 'up' means the conquest of more
territory and thus one finally gets ahead anyway .
. . When the moment (the beginning of a real class
struggle) has come, everything will happen
tremendously fast and energetically over there.
But this might not come to pass for quite some
time. Miracles do not happen anywhere . . . only
great events can be of any help. If in addition
to the transfer of national land to private land
ownership (a process which is almost completed)
industry will expand under a less crazy tariff
policy, and if the foreign markets will be
conquered, conditions in your country might indeed
improve. . . . It is the revolutionizing of all
traditional conditions by developing industry
which also revolutionizes the mind!

Chapter VIII: Endnotes

[1]The general later admitted before the
investigation committee that he had made such a
statement.

9
The Report on the Chicago Strike of June–July 1894 by the United States Strike Commission

The last congressional elections (November 1894), which had been so disastrous for the Democratic Party, were hardly over when the Report on the Chicago Strike by the United States Strike Commission appeared; its content created a sensation and caused the purely capitalist bourgeois press to hurl furious insults against its authors. Besides the facts and eye witness accounts (reproduced with laudable frankness and veracity) which are a devastating indictment of the employers (Pullman and allied railroads) and which tear the mask of labor-philia from the faces of the big industrialists, the report contains a plethora of petit-bourgeois phrases and philanthropic tirades that petit-bourgeois citizens, small peasants and reformers like to employ against big capital. Excerpts are given here of the most important and interesting parts. Repetitions of what has been reported earlier in the Neue Zeit have been avoided. The widespread sentimental, philanthropic and moral sermons have been abbreviated whenever possible, whereas the loquacious and garrulous style could not always be eliminated. So that those that possess the original document may easily consult and compare it to the excerpts, the original organization of the material, even at the cost of being less, has been strictly adhered to.

After a copy of the letter which the committee submitted with its report to the president, and after a citation of the laws under which the committee was appointed, follows yet an address of the chairman, C.D. Wright, to the spectators and participants who had appeared for the opening of the investigations. Then the report itself follows.

The committee met for 13 days at Chicago, it listened to 109 witnesses (107 in Chicago and 2 in

Washington), and it came to the conclusion that the
battle had been chiefly between the American Railway
Union and the General Managers' Association.

The loss of the allied railroads as to
property, salaries for auxiliary sheriffs
and other expenditures amounted to at
least: $685,308
Their loss of revenue due to the
suspension of work: $4,672,916
About 3100 Pullman employees lost
in wages at least: $ 350,000
About 100,000 railroad employees
lost in wages at least: $1,389,143

Many of these employees are still today without
work and wages. The battlefield report reads as
follows:

Shot and mortally wounded: 12 Persons
Arrested by the police: 575 Persons
Arrested and indicted
     under federal laws: 71 Persons
Arrested, but not indicted: 119 Persons

The forces sent to suppress the insurrection were:
United States troops sent to Chicago
     between July 3rd and July 10th
     and used there: 1936 Men
National Guard put into service
     at Chicago: about   4000 Men
Extra Auxiliary Marshals
     (U.S. officials):   about   5000 Men
Extra Auxiliary Sheriffs
     (state officials):   about   280 Men
Police from Chicago   3000 Men
                    Altogether: 14,186 Men

        Certainly not unintentionally, the report goes on
to cite the article of the constitution which assures
every state the protection of the federal government
against internal unrest and rebellion if the legislature
or the governor wants to make use of the protection.
Under this article, the president had no right to allow
troops to move into the city, but subsequently two
paragraphs of the federal laws are cited which give the
president this power under certain circumstances without
regard to the governor or the legislature.
        The report gives the same description about the
Pullman Palace Car Company and the town that appeared in
the Neue Zeit. The beautiful church, the parks, the
library, etc., in Pullman are mentioned, and then it is
stated:

"... The company employs a doctor who is
also a surgeon, and pays him an annual salary in
order that he may treat injured employees and give
them the necessary medicine. However, it is also
one of his duties to obtain from the injured a
written statement about the causes of the accident
and then to put them under pressure to accept a
settlement or indemnity. If the matter comes
before a court, the doctor usually appears as a
witness for the company. . . ."

As a result of the Pullman system and its growth,
the committee finds at the beginning of the crisis in
1893 that:

"... On the one hand, there is a very rich and
unyielding body, and on the other hand, there is a
mass of workers of relatively sterling character
and skill but without special interest and
responsibility for the town, its administration,
its buildings and environment. The conditions
which have been created at Pullman allow the
directors of the company at any time to assert
their assumed right to determine the wages and
rents and to suppress any urge for independence
which causes workers to found organizations to
initiate mediation, employ compulsory arbitration,
declare and lead strikes and so on. . . ."

The report then goes on to describe the creation of
the American Railway Union, gives excerpts from its
constitution, praises it but regrets that it does not
contain a paragraph to punish or exclude members that
commit or advise violence. The following sentence
criticizes the Pullman Company for refusing to recognize
the labor organizations: "In this respect, the Pullman
Company is behind the age."
The American Railway Union is advised to strike
only as a last resort, and the following urgent
recommendations are made for it:

"Conservative leadership, legal
incorporation, education of its members by the
study of governmental affairs while observing the
principle that in this country labor can only
achieve protection and removal of injustices by
conservative progress (sic!), legal conduct and
wise laws, which are maintained by the public
opinions of the actual ruler: the people."

Of the General Managers' Association it is reported
that it was founded in 1886 and that it includes all
railroads which have their center or terminate in
Chicago.

"The operation of these railroads extends over
40,933 miles. The number of shareholders amounts
to 52,088."

Capitalization

The Share Capital. . . . . $ 818,596,004
The Funded Debt. 1,210,235,702
The Current (Floating) Debt.   9,747,911
                                       $2,108,552,617

The Gross Income during the past fiscal year:
$325,825,726
The Net Income during the past fiscal year:
102,701,917
The number of employees was 221,097 persons."

The president of the General Managers' Association
states that this association will be able and has always
been able to draw people together at Chicago through its
various agencies in order to be prepared for all
eventualities. In November 1894, the association sent a
uniform pay roll to all 24 members, whereupon various
train companies carried out wage reductions. The
committee calls this procedure "an usurpation" because
the General Managers' Association has no license and no
rights of corporation: "The conduct of the General
Managers' Association illustrates the continuous and
calculated plans of the companies to augment their power
and indirectly to usurp rights and privileges which are
not contained in their permits and which are
unobtainable from the people and the legislatures." If
this should continue, the railroads and the government
will confront each other and then will certainly occur
the nationalization of the railroads." The refusal of
the General Managers' Association to recognize and to
negotiate with a labor organization such as the American
Railway Union is arrogant and in the view of its
position vis-a-vis the law, its usurpations and its past
as well as evidently its future behavior--absurd.

The committee describes the conduct of the
officials of the Pullman Company towards their workers
as far as wages rents are concerned in practically the
same way as the Neue Zeit earlier this year. It points
to the testimonies of witnesses and the stereotype
answer of the company to the demands for mediation or
compulsory arbitration that "there is nothing to
arbitrate." The report confirms that the rents for
apartments in Pullman are 20 to 25% higher than for
similar housing in Chicago or neighboring towns. A
favorite capitalist saying is dismissed as follows:

"In the declarations to the audience, the
(Pullman) Company asserted that all of its actions

were solely motivated by the desire to keep the
business going in order to help the workers and
the businessmen in and around Pullman, and in
order to protect the public from the inconvenience
growing out of an interrupted train traffic.
Basing itself upon the testimonies of witnesses
the committee, however, is of the opinion that the
company tried to conduct its business primarily
for its own advantage so that its factories and
workshops would suffer no damage by non-usage, so
that no competitors might enter the field, so that
they could keep their railroad cars in tact, so
that they could be ready as soon as business
revived to resume work with undamaged machinery
and skillful workers and in order to collect their
income from rents in an undiminished fashion."

The refusal of the company to reduce rents along
with wages is criticized and the strikers are praised
for their dignified behavior as well as the fact that no
violence and no destruction of property took place while
they guarded the plants (May 4th until July 3rd).
The report furthermore describes the attempts at
mediation which were made on July 13th (by the city
council, the mayor and others) and adds:

"The policy of the Pullman Company and the
General Managers' Association in regard to the
attempts to solve the conflict by arbitration
prevented from the very beginning all efforts to
mediate the quarrel and achieve a reconciliation.
The committee has been convinced by the
testimonies of witnesses as well as newly revealed
details, that different policies (of the above-
mentioned) would have prevented the great loss of
life, property and wages resulting from the
strike."

The extraordinary activity of the General Managers"
Association is described:

". . . The General Managers' Association met
daily in order to receive reports and in order to
take the necessary measures. Constant
communications were maintained with the bourgeois
and military offices in regard to troop
detachments and police movements, auxiliary
marshals and soldiers."

From the riotous scenes in Chicago, it reports:

"Among the mobs were also many objectionable
foreigners who have been thrust upon us by the
unlimited immigration policy."

Of the police and soldiers it is reported:

"The policemen undoubtedly sympathized more
with the strikers than the train companies, and it
would not be surprising at all if similar feelings
reigned among the soldiers. Most of the ordinary
soldiers had been recruited from the working
class. Indeed, the danger increases that during
future hostilities between employers and employees
the necessary war duty will in the end no longer
be carried out by volunteers from the working
class but by other folks."
"3600 auxiliary marshals (federal employers)
were selected and appointed upon the request of
the General Managers' Association. They were
armed and paid by the railroads and acted thus in
the double capacity of railroad employees and
officials of the United States. . . . This placed
government officials under the control of the
railroads and established an evil precedent that
could easily lead to dangerous consequences.
. . ."
"The mobs which after July 3rd occupied
stations, tracks and crossings, toppled railroad
carriages, burnt, destroyed and robbed were,
according to the unanimous testimony of witnesses,
bums and women of the lowest class of foreigners
[what's meant here is immigrants] and recruits
from the criminal class. Very few strikers were
noticed and recognized among them and very few
were arrested. . . . "

Of the competition, which is always praised as a
means for preventing a single enterprise from becoming
predominant, the committee states:

"Among the 24 railroad companies who have
joined forces, all competition for workers has
ceased. On the other hand, the competition among
their workers grows stronger all the time. The
competition among the railroads has long been
stopped by the cartels and conglomerates. . . .
The legislation concerning interstate commerce and
the railroad commission in more than 30 states is
described as the result of the people's efforts to
protect themselves from the cessation of
competition as produced by the cartels. . . . The
growth of associated wealth and its power is the
astonishing achievement of the last 50 years. The
corporations have undoubtedly helped the country
by exploring its resources and making them
available to us all. It should not come as a
surprise at all if the growth of labor to equal
power and responsibility will become the miracle

(the achievement of development) of the next fifty
years!"

Many suggestions were made to the committee by
various people, suggestions designed to ameliorate the
strife between labor and capital. The list is long:
"Government control or nationalization of the railroads,
compulsory arbitration, licensing (employment by
examination) of employees, the introduction of a single
tax (abolition of all other tariffs and levies) on real
estate, limitation of immigration and exclusion of
paupers, tariffs for American industries, currency and
coinage legislation, the suppression of trusts and
cartels, written contracts dealing with dismissal or
firing, the creation of a United States Labor Committee
to investigate and set working hours and wages, the
empowering of the courts to solve these questions,
insurance and pensions for employees, legal
determination of the working hours and a minimum wage,
determination of a work unit (just as there are units
for weight, measurements, etc.), legal liability of
employers vis-a-vis their employees and various moral
recommendations."

"When the railroads still acted without
restrictions and as they pleased towards their clients,
the people demanded a tribunal that would deal justly
with both parties, and Congress agreed to that: In view
of the Chicago insurrection and the dangers that have
been evoked by it, the people have the same right to
establish a federal committee to investigate and report
the quarrels between the railroads and its employees in
order that the public order and business will be less
disturbed by strikes and boycotts. . . . Since the
railroads can hardly be considered as individuals or
private corporations but, in a certain sense, must be
viewed as public corporations which have been forced by
the state and which, for public purposes, were given
certain rights, they may then be compelled to follow the
decisions of the proposed federal committee, even if the
workers cannot be compelled to obey in a similar
fashion. It would certainly be in the public interest
if the railroads would not be allowed to stop their
services during strife with labor, etc."

The committee closes its report with three
recommendations: I to Congress, II to the individual
states and III to the employers.

I. To the Congress

1. Similar to the Inter-State Commerce Commission, a
permanent Federal Strike Commission of three members
should be formed, that is obligated and empowered to
investigate the disputes between the railroads and its
employees and to hand in reports concerning them.

a. Just as in the case of the inter-state trade
law, the federal courts will be empowered to force
the railroads by summary action, freed of all
technical formalities, to follow the decisions of
the strike commission and to allow no delay by a
possible appeal.

b. If in the case of a dispute before the
commission, one or more railroads confront one or
more federally or state incorporated unions, then
each party should have the right to elect a
representative that will be appointed by the
President as a temporary member of the commission
for the resolving of the respective case.

(This proposal would arouse interest in the
labor organization for legal incorporation,
and it would give the commission the
character of a mediation office and obtain
trust for this body and supply practical
knowledge from both sides.)

c. After a national union or incorporated labor
organization has started legal proceedings before
the commission, it should be illegal for the
railroads to dismiss employees, unless in case of
inability, negligence or the violation of the law.
It should be equally illegal for the concerned
unions and organizations to declare, further or
favor strikes or boycotts against the accused
railroads during such a proceeding. It should,
furthermore, be illegal for the railroads within
six months after a decision, to dismiss employees
and to replace them with other people, except for
the above-mentioned reasons. It should also be
illegal for employees to quit their services
during the same time period without giving a
written notice 30 days prior to their intended
resignation, and it should be illegal for the
concerned union or organization to make decisions
that deviate from these decrees.

2. Chapter 567 of the laws of the United States for the
years 1885-86 should be amended to read that the
national labor unions will be made to announce in their
statutes, rules and by-laws, that any member will lose
his rights and his membership if he commits or causes
others to commit violence against persons or property
during strikes and boycotts or if he uses force, threats
or intimidation to keep others from working. In
addition, members of such unions will be no more
personally liable and responsible for corporate actions
than the shareholders of a corporation, etc.

3. The committee has not been able to consider
sufficiently the question of licensing the railroads to
make any recommendations, but it advises earnestly and
urgently that a proper congressional committee should
make a careful and comprehensive study of this matter.

II. To the Individual States

1. The committee would like to recommend to the
individual states the adoption of a mediation and
arbitration system similar to the one that exists in
Massachusetts. The system could be improved and
strengthened by amendments that would give the mediation
committee greater power by permitting it to investigate
all strikes--whether asked to do so or not. It should
be considered whether labor organizations should not be
given the same legal rights as those that have been
proposed for the national labor unions.

2. Contracts which oblige workers not to join a union
or, if the case requires, to leave one, as a condition
for their employment, ought to be declared illegal as
has already happened in several states.

III. To the Employers

1. The committee asks the employers urgently to
recognize the labor organizations and to negotiate with
their representatives.

Chapter IX: Endnotes

[1] Among the shareholders are thousands of little people who possess perhaps between 1 to 10 shares. A large number of those shares are valued between 7 to 30 dollars a share. Many of these railroads have not paid any interest for years.

10
The Annual Convention of the Knights of Labor and the American Federation of Labor

On November 13th, 1894, the annual General Assembly of the Knights of Labor was opened in New Orleans. About 75 delegates had appeared, among them a considerable number of Socialists. The annual message of the new Grand Master Workman, Sovereign, stresses the aim of the order which is the abolition of the wage system and the creation of a co-operative system of industry. It recalls the manly support given by the Knights of Labor to the American Railway Union last summer during its memorable battle; it sharply attacks any augmentation of the standing army and its use to suppress the workers. Otherwise, however, the message stresses the opposition of the Knights of Labor to the gold loans of the government, its ties to the Farmers' Union, the Populist and similar outfits, and as a new addition to the Declaration of Principles of the Order, the Grand Master Workman proposes: "that sales based on installment payments and speculation with farm products and other vital necessities ought to be regarded as criminal, declared illegal and properly punished."

An attempt by the former General Master Workman, T. V. Powderly, to stage a come-back, was defeated. For purely formal reasons it was decided, after a vehement debate, not to admit the various miner organizations' representatives--a decision which created much dissatisfaction. It was decided to continue energetically the fight against gold loans and for silver (16:1) and to agitate for the referendum and the initiative.

The socialists seemed to have little influence. In general, the order recommends independent political action as a matter of principle, but the word "independent" is interpreted in such a way that it only means independent of both of the parties (Republican and

Democratic). The Order maintains close ties to the
Farmer Unionists and the Populists.

There is no doubt that the Order has suffered a
great loss in membership and esteem.

The attention of this country's workers was
primarily concentrated last year upon the Annual
Convention of the American Federation of Labor which met
at Denver, Colorado on December 11th and dealt with the
well-known Plank 10 (collective ownership of the means
of production) as well as the creation of an independent
political workers' party. Interest was heightened by
the appearance of two delegates from the Parliamentary
Committee of the British Trade Union Congress, John
Burns and David Holms. All year long, the possible
entry of the union into the political arena and Plank 10
were eagerly discussed, but the advocates (as well as
the opponents) of the new tactics and policies were
uncertain as to the outcome. Experts on the situation,
however, predicted that the very fact that the congress
was being held in the Far West, away from the great
industrial centers of the land, boded ill for the "new
departure."

President Gompers' "address," his Annual Message,
was very long. Its most important points will be
reported and discussed in the following paragraphs.

Of the miners' strike it is reported that 125,000
workers participated, that it lasted eight weeks and
ended in a compromise: the establishment of a minimum
wage.

The strike of the American Railway Union, the so-
called Pullman Strike, is described and the activity (it
should be called inactivity) of the executive of the AFL
is related and a vote of confidence for the executive is
asked for because it had been heavily criticized. On
July 9th (that is thirteen days after the boycott
declaration and six days after the federal troops
marched into Chicago) he (President Gompers) had
received a dispatch asking him to come immediately to
Chicago. "It seemed to me both unwise and impractical,
be it as an individual or be it as president of the AFL,
to go to Chicago because I could not take any tangible
official action. . . . So I convoked a session of the
Executive Committee at Chicago to which I also invited
the leading officials of the other great unions . . . "

As is well known, the result of this conference was
zero. President Gompers may be right when he remarks
that he did not have sufficient authority, but he
forgets: statutes and by-laws cannot foresee
everything. Certain moments come and situations arise
when one has to act without being a stickler for the
letter of the law. The officials of such a respected
and influential group as the AFL should not grow stale
and then sink into a bureaucratic swamp, but if the
necessity arises, they must be willing to act as

officers and army leaders. It is not proper for them to
take a back seat all the time and to wait until they are
called. At the reception for John Burns, Samuel Gompers
repeatedly and rightfully praised and eulogized the
English guest as "the hero of Trafalgar Square" but the
applause which followed that description would have been
drowned out by thousandfold jubilation if Burns could
have responded to the compliment by calling Gompers "the
hero of the Chicago Strike" or some such phrase.

The message said a lot about the immigration of
indentured workers. This subject is not very important
nowadays because there is more emigration than
immigration. Not exactly nice, and hardly fitting the
president of the AFL, is the recommendation to hire
secret police to travel across the sea in steerage in
order to investigate the immigrants.

The miserable treatment of sailors on American
ships is criticized, and steps to remedy the situation
are recommended.

Labor Day on the first Monday in September has been
declared a national holiday by resolution of Congress--
"the only ray of light of the entire legislation of the
past session of Congress."

The report that the agitation for bi-metalism on
the basis of 16:1 had been furthered, confirms a retreat
of the worst kind, of which the AFL had not been thought
capable.

The negotiations with the Knights of Labor have not
led to any acceptable results and the Annual Message
declares that there cannot be two authorities and two
organizations in the unions. This passage is clearly
directed against the Knights of Labor who possess
respectable organizations in various unions.

The message came out strongly against compulsory
arbitration, prophesied the resurgence of industry
within a year and thanked the British Trade Union
Congress for sending two delegates whose presence "has
honored the AFL beyond measure."

The unions from California demanded that the
Congress of the United States should cease to make any
further concessions to the Union and Central Pacific
Railroad Companies' in regard to the immense debts that
they owe to the United States. Instead these railroads
should be simply taken over as the first recommendable
step towards their eventual nationalization. The
president and the executive committee did not comment on
this question but left it up to the convention.

As far as the Eight-Hour Movement is concerned, the
Annual Report recommends that a new push should be
undertaken to obtain the Eight-Hour Law and to extend it
to all government employees. Demands were made for the
abolition of contract work as well as the legal
limitation of the work of women and children to eight
hours a day.

About the most important proposal, the creation of an independent political movement of the workers and the program to be designed in connection with it under Plank 10, President Gompers said among other things:

" . . . A number of demands which are contained in the program have been made by nearly all of the unions of the world, but they contain an innocent appearing and almost hidden declaration which not only has been heavily contested but is purely theoretical; and even if it should rest on economic verities, these are not demonstrable and are remote so that they will put us and our movement into an unenviable light. If our organization should become identified with it, many capable national labor unions will be dissuaded from joining our ranks and fighting with us to attain first things first. It is ridiculous to imagine that wage workers can gain power at the ballot while they are slaves at work. So far it has never happened that autocracy in the factory and democracy in the political sphere have existed contemporaneously and side by side. In reality, we have not even attained the first step towards controlling public affairs: the recognition of our unions."

He then talked about the action of the organized workers of Great Britain who formed a committee to further working class interests in parliament, and he recommended to the American workers that they follow this example. He also referred to the former National Labor Union that supposedly perished because it became involved in the electoral process. He said furthermore:

"Before we may hope to enter the arena with a general organization that puts up its own candidates, the workers must be more extensively organized, and better results must be obtained in local experiments. No political workers' movement can and will succeed upon the wreckage of the labor union movement. . . . "

It is a duty to raise objections and to criticize the above-mentioned remarks which carry an official seal of approval. To label Plank 10 "innocent appearing and almost hidden" is a bit thick and obviously contradicted by the fact that it was discussed for an entire year by all labor newspapers and labor leagues. The demand is "not demonstrable"? Proof, however, cannot be adduced without demonstration by practice, by trying it out. The claim that the demand is "remote" is amply counterbalanced by the adjacent misery of the wage workers. It is true that already today a fifth of all

wage workers have been either entirely or partially
thrown out into the street by the development of
technology and machines. Is the proletariat supposed to
wait with the seizure of the machinery, etc. until half
or two-thirds of its members are without work and also,
of course, in such misery that they can no longer stage
rational initiatives but only starvation riots? If the
wage workers "cannot gain power at the ballot" as long
as they are "slaves at work"--should their slavery then
be eternalized? Should not the slaves rather be spurred
on to become conscious of their situation and to try to
improve it with the encouragement of their co-workers?

By the way, the sentence "autocracy in the factory
and democracy in the political sphere have never existed
contemporaneously" is just as accurate as its reverse:
"Democracy in the factory and autocracy in the political
sphere" cannot exist side by side.

The situation of the workers in the United States
needs improvement and guarantees against deterioration,
and the wage workers who are spearheading the class
struggle (and to which up until now belonged the AFL in
a prominent position) must assault the bulwarks of
bourgeois exploitation and even the bourgeoisie itself.
After all, Gompers himself remarked at the end,
regarding the program:

> "We require an all-encompassing overview of
> the arena, an acute judgment, wise and well-
> considered advice and aggressive action."

It is always opportune to go over to the attack,
but one has to know where, when and how. To determine
the route of the march, the timing and the nature of the
attack, is up to the labor parliament, whereas the
details, the disposition of the forces and the supplies,
are the business of the officials and leaders. The
Annual Message also refers to the fact that the former
National Labor Union entered the electoral battle of
1872, put up candidates and never held a convention
again, i.e., it was destroyed by its participation.
This claim contains serious errors. The only true
assertion is that the National Labor Union did put up
candidates in 1872, but it is equally true that the
National Labor Union was no longer a labor organization
at that time but a group of petit-bourgeois reformers.
The National Labor Union was destroyed by 1872 or even
earlier by the greenback humbug whose equivalent today
is the silver humbug. Whoever of the old greenback
leaders and politicians is still alive is active for
silver today just as he was rooting for greenbacks
twenty-five years ago. With the growth of the greenback
movement and its penetration of the National Labor
Union, the aspirations of the working class became
falsified. Thus started the decay of the National Labor

Union which may be easily documented by the still
available lists of participants of the congresses. The
labor unions withdrew and by 1870 already, the majority
of the congress at Cincinnati was non-union. The last
congress of the National Labor Union took place in 1874
at Rochester, New York. It is exactly the fate of the
National Labor Union which should serve as a warning
example to the American Federation of Labor so that it
will ward off petit-bourgeois and reformist elements and
experiments and will throw overboard the silver humbug
and similar stuff.

If the Annual Report expresses its opposition to
universal (country-wide) elections before "better
organizations" and "better results in local experiments
have been achieved," then one can only whole heartedly
express one's approval. Even the firebrands of the
electoral movement should take this advice to heart.
But--a beginning must be made somewhere and one should
undertake local experiments. As far as the Eight Hour
Question is concerned, the AFL has always been willing
to abandon the general demands in order to attack
individual points, and it has thus achieved remarkable
successes. Very well, let it proceed in the same manner
as far as the political movement is concerned. Let it
designate a state, a district or a city as the
battlefield and concentrate all of its available
resources and manpower there. Let it continue its
efforts there until it is put into a position to attack
and conquer larger regions.

That a parliamentary committee for the guarding and
influencing of legislation (similar to the one in
England) has been appointed is most laudable, and one
can only hope that this similarity is not reflected in
its activity, i.e., the intensity of it. Greater
effectiveness and greater diligence are to be
recommended to the American parliamentary committee. For
years now, individual large labor unions, as for
example, the Cigar Makers, the Typographers, the
Sailors, etc., have sought to represent their interests
in congress by permanent or temporary committees, and it
has been a serious sin of omission by the AFL not to
have instituted long ago a permanent lobby for labor
interests in congress.

Last year's revenues of the AFL amounted to
$22,493.87 and the expenditures were $17,302.08 (among
the latter were considerable donations to hard-pressed
unions).

The debates over Plank 10 and all that was
connected with it were hot and heavy and lasted for two
days. Parliamentary as well as extra-parliamentary
tricks were employed to defeat the Plank. For example,
the introduction to the program which deals with the
British labor movement and its Trade Union Congress was
attacked and rejected, whereupon certain delegates

declared themselves freed of their instructions or imperative mandates to vote for an independent labor electoral movement and Plank 10. They then voted against it. Plank 10 was rejected, or rather emasculated, when its place was taken by a plank opposing land monopoly. The independent electoral movement was thus, for the time being, laid ad acta.[2]

The recommendations contained in the Annual Report were mostly accepted: the demand of the California unions in respect to the Pacific railroads; the extension of the Eight Hour Work Law for women and children, as it exists in Illinois, to all states; the abolition of manual work and the sweat shops; legal restrictions on the nonsense of judicial injunctions; legal recognition of the trademarks of labor unions; abolition of all conspiracy laws that are directed against workers; abolition of the patron system which is particularly wide-spread among the Italians; etc., etc. It was decided to make another try (starting on May 1st, 1896) to achieve the Eight Hour Day. Negotiations with the Knights of Labor were only to be held if these people would come out against the duplication of organization and authority in all unions. It was decided to send S. Gompers and P. J. McGuire to the next trade union congress in England (Cardiff), to protest against compulsory arbitration as well as against the issuance of new debt certificates (loans) by the government except by special law of the Congress of the United States.

With the exception of the first vice-president and the treasurer, an entirely new executive committee was chosen. John McBride of the miners replaced Gompers as president, and the executive's seat was moved to Indianapolis.

To allude to the retrogressive steps reflected in the resolution of the convention is not necessary after the remarks which have already been made about the annual message. But even here in these pure formalities, the retrogression is unmistakable. Gompers has never identified himself with the old bourgeois parties, and he has never played a role in them, which cannot be said of his successor John McBride who achieved worthy accomplishments for a number of years as labor statistician of the State of Ohio but, in contrast, accomplished very little during last year's great miners' strike.

The transfer of the headquarters of the AFL to Indianapolis, Indiana, is a big mistake because it cuts off the contact of the executive with a warm, pulsating life of a great industrial and commercial center. Such contact is vital for the officials of a labor movement. New York or Chicago ought to be the seat of the AFL, given today's conditions.

Chapter X: Endnotes

[1]The railroads were originally built with the government money, credit and land, i.e., they have received money, interest guarantees and immense land from the government of the United States under the condition that they would make interest payments beginning in 1895.

[2]John Burns was absent during this debate in the convention, but he is supposed to have called the enemies of Plank 10 "asses".

11
The Strike in Brooklyn and Other Events

The strike of the American Railway Union (Chicago) has left its subsequent traces upon the ruling class and the bourgeoisie of the United States, and it has born corresponding fruits.

President Cleveland stated in his message to congress, at the beginning of last December, in a somewhat irritated tone: "It is hardly necessary to recall the fact that in pursuit of constitutional and legal commandments and for the protection of the property of the United States, as well as to assist the federal courts and to remove illegal obstacles to the exercise of the legitimate functions of the government, it became necessary during the course of the year to use at different places a significant part of the regular troops." He praised the courage and the precision of the officers and soldiers, called for a considerable increase of the standing army in view of "recent events," mentioned the withdrawal of various small army posts in conformity with "the policy of concentrating the army at the important centers of population and transportation" and mentioned several times the smallness of the available forces.

The commanding general of the army spoke more frankly in his annual report in which he demanded an increase of the standing army and justified it with the following words: "More than once, a furious mob (rebellious multitude) of a single town was twice as strong numerically and twice as capable to destroy life and property as the largest and worst league of Indian warriors that ever defied the army of this country. In

other words: the army has recently found it necessary
to turn upon an enemy who is more numerous and more
dangerous to the country than all the savages that it
had to fight until now."
    Examples have been given in earlier reports of the
comments of the bourgeois press. It was now the turn of
the official representatives of education at the various
universities of the country to hurry up and prove their
correct sentiments. For about fifteen to twenty years,
there have been economics and political science
professors at the different institutes of higher
learning in the United States who have not been inimical
to socialism and at times have even been tinged with
this ideology. Many of them have been educated in
Germany and their articles appeared in many general as
well as scholarly periodicals. During the Great Strike
of Chicago, their names disappeared from these
publications as if a boycott had been initiated against
them. Professor R. T. Ely, who has often been mentioned
in the Neue Zeit, had to face a trial because of heresy,
i.e., favoring workers' demands as well as teaching
socialist doctrines. He was freed of all charges after
Mr. Ely's colleagues testified as to his good character.
    How the courts behaved towards the strike of the
railroad employees has been amply described. What has
to be added now is the fact that Debs and various other
members of the directorate of the American Railway Union
were convicted last year in Chicago on December 14th to
six months in jail--not because of any illegal acts but
because of contempt of court. They have recently begun
to serve their sentence. An appeal was made to the
highest court of the country (The Supreme Court of the
United States) and this court ordered the release of the
accused during the legal proceedings on $2,000 bail.
Similar sentences were handed out in several towns of
the country, and in California a participant of last
year's railroad strike was condemned to death after
having been accused of having caused a train derailment
which resulted in death and injury to several people.
    The president and the press, professors and
provosts all shouted unanimously: vae victis!
    The well-known Governor Altgeld gave a superb
epilogue directed to the president, his ministers and
the federal judges, in the form of his annual message to
the Illinois legislature in which he labeled the conduct
of the government during the strike in Chicago as
"government by injunction" which he castigated.
    The Eastern industrial states are in turmoil. The
wage reductions, which have been going on since the
summer of 1893, have lowered the workers' standard of
living to such an extent that even the most patient ones
are becoming angry and restless. The previously
reported significant strikes of the weavers and spinners
in New Bedford, Fall River and other towns of

Massachusetts, New Hampshire and Rhode Island, lasted
for quite some time but did not end favorably for the
workers as a whole as there are continuous new quarrels
between the workers and their employers. The latter
showed no desire to give in because many of the great
enterprises are getting ready to emigrate, i.e., their
factories are heading south, especially to Georgia and
Alabama, because cotton and coal happen to be nearer at
hand there, and there are also cheaper and more
submissive workers (blacks, women and children). This
transfer has already progressed to such an extent that
the more significant daily newspapers maintain a column
entitled "The Cotton Mills in the South." The chief
reason for this factory migration and colonization is
the meekness and tolerance that the southern states show
toward the factory owners' dealings with the workers.
There is greater freedom from the type of governmental
intervention, particularly intervention in favor of the
workers, which happens more or less frequently to the
employers in the New England states (in other words:
the bigger or smaller lack of labor protective laws in
the southern states of the country). A genuine
capitalist paper reports about the intended transfer of
three important factories and lists the causes: the
first reason is that they can produce cheaper there
because the raw materials are closer at hand, and the
coal supplies are also much closer so that considerable
money can be saved because they do not have to be
transported from afar. In addition, there is the
cheaper price of labor in the South and . . . the fear
of hostile (hostile to the employer) labor protective
legislation in the North.
     The labor statistician of North Carolina writes as
follows about the lack of labor protective legislation.
"A large number of cotton manufacturers and workers in
this state should feel the arm of the law, and the
legislature will be asked to issue a number of laws
concerning the employment and treatment of workers in
the cotton mills." A worker who pursues this affair
(before the legislature) writes about it: "I am
speaking on behalf of the women and children who have to
work every week 72 hours in many of the cotton and wool
factories of this state. As I understand, there is no
other state in the union where the working hours amount
to more than 11 hours a day. The black lays his tiles,
carries his mortar, pushes his plane, swings his axe and
drives his team for 10 hours, then his work day has
concluded. The white artisan begins his work at 7
o'clock in the morning, takes an hour break and returns
to his family at 7 p.m., but the workers in the cotton
factory (for the most part women and children) have to
eat their breakfast at 6 a.m., their lunch break amounts
usually only to 40 minutes, and they have to work until
7 p.m. Foreigners (immigrants) in the factories of the

North, in New England and the West work only 10 hours.
In South Carolina, Tennessee, Georgia, and Alabama, the
workday consists of 11 hours. Only the women and
children of the factories of North Carolina have to work
more than 12 hours a day. The last legislature was
asked for protective labor laws, but the proposed
measures were not adopted because the majority of the
factory owners remonstrated against them. It was even
said: "We do not want labor legislation at this time
when so much Northern capital wants to invest in the
South. We want to see this Northern capital invested
here and the agitation over factory work might chase it
away! Nevertheless, renewed (and hopefully successful)
efforts will be made in order to obtain laws concerning
the working hours in cotton mills as well as the age of
children who are employed there and the amount of their
working hours."

Among the shoeworkers in Massachusetts there has
long been great dissatisfaction over working conditions
and wages, and in Haverhill (and in other towns), a
strike broke out because of that, a strike that
virtually paralyzed most of the factories. But
"government, by injunction" has also caught on in New
England, and the state courts are being urged to issue
injunctions against the strikers--which they are more
than willing to do even if it is not done in such an
all-encompassing manner as in the case of the gentlemen
Dagro, Perkins, Grosscup and accomplices. The business
is not yet concluded.

Last autumn, a significant and interesting fight
broke out in New York between the cloakmakers and their
exploiters, a fight which was significant due to the
large number (around 8,000) of the participating workers
and the interesting peculiarities connected with it.
With few exceptions, all participants, the exploited as
well as the exploiters, the workers, the contractors and
the employers all belonged to the Jewish race.
Intriguers were heavily involved and the rivalry between
the Knights of Labor and the open unions played an
important part at first. The New York police
department, which at that very moment was being indicted
by an investigating committee of the legislature, vented
its wrath upon the workers by the brutal beating of a
crowd that was getting ready to demonstrate. The
endurance and self-sacrifice of the Jewish workers was
admirable. They bore their sufferings and privations
without complaining and without relinquishing their
demands, and in the end, the philanthropic societies
felt compelled to offer help to the starving strikers.
The street cleaning commissioner wanted to employ the
strikers for snow and ice removal, but he was prevented
from doing so by a law which had been passed by the
legislature the year before last which allows only
citizens (native-born or naturalized) to work in public

jobs. The cloakmakers' season is close at hand, and it
is likely that the exploiters will make small
concessions now so that the strikers will resume their
work and the employers will "do business" once again.
   With the new year, the tailors' cutters of New York
also put in their appearance, closed their ranks and
began a fight over the Eight Hour Work Schedule which
had been forced upon them by improved techniques.
   The most important event, however, which has
strongly aroused all segments of the urban population is
the strike of the street car employees in Brooklyn, the
sister city of New York.
   The workers of the electricity-driven street cars
of Brooklyn were already negotiating last fall with
their employers about an improvement of their situation
and the removal of various bad conditions. The
negotiations dragged on for a long time but were broken
off at the beginning of this year because the train
administration did not want to agree to anything;
whereupon the well-organized good workers, who all
belonged to the order of the Knights of Labor, struck on
January 14th. With the exception of the steam-operated
elevated trains, which run on pillars, all trains
stopped running and the good citizens and inhabitants of
the church town felt uneasy. The "citizens" and
businessmen demanded the restoration of the regular
service; the train administration tried to hire scabs in
every possible way and asserted that there was not
enough police protection to resume service; the mayor, a
German Philistine and reformer of the finest capitalist
kind, scratched his head to find an expedient or
panacea; the police commissioner mobilized his entire
force and occupied all of the points of departure and
the terminals of the trains--but the strikers laughed up
their sleeves because the trains were not running due to
the lack of skilled personnel. One of the most
important train administrations now made an acceptable
compromise with the workers (and, in the meantime, a
good business deal), whereas the other administrators
only shouted for more police and soldiers. The mayor
was touched by the suffering of the train shareholders
and officials and called out the city's National Guard
units. This action, too, did not obtain any scabs for
the train presidents so the entire National Guard of New
York City was called upon to help on January 20th. This
changed the whole situation for the worse because of
unprovoked and unexpected beatings, thrashings,
stabbings and shootings on the part of the Guards. In
order to convey a graphic picture of the strike, I will
reproduce here a number of excerpts from a strictly (and
even aggressively) capitalist paper dated January 22nd
to January 26th of this year. For a better
understanding of these reports, it should be pointed out
that Brooklyn (New York State) covers an enormous

territory and, therefore, maintains an enormous
streetcar network and that most of the incorporated
towns (like Ridgewood, Flatbush, etc.) are still called
by those names just as before their incorporation. Ave.
stands for Avenue and St. for Street. Before the
intervention of the Guard, law and order was not
disturbed in Brooklyn.

January 22nd: "In general, the citizens of
Brooklyn are of the opinion that the city's authorities,
including the police, have more sympathy for the
strikers than is normal these days. The arrival of New
York's troops (Guard) has modified this opinion
somewhat, but many a life may be lost before the mob
will realize that the First Brigade (of New York City)
did not move out for the fun of it. The men have been
seriously provoked.

Colonel Appleton of the 7th Regiment came out with
an Order of the Day this morning in which he calls upon
his men to make use of their weapons as soon as objects
are thrown at them.

In the darkness (the police do not know when),
wires were cut along Gates Ave. and Myrtle Ave.

In Ridgewood everything has been paralyzed. Four
trolley lines originate from there: Gates Ave., Myrtle
Ave., Bashwick Ave. and Knickerbocker Ave., as well as
three steam-driven lines to Richmond, Cypresshill and
the Lutheran Cemetery. Not a single train passed along
the lines today. . . . At 7:30 the attempt was made to
repair the cut wires. When the people arrived at the
first place that they were supposed to fix, the strikers
persuaded them not to repair anything; they quit work,
dropped their tools and joined the strikers.

Later it was decided to try to repair the wires
under police protection. These repairs are needed most
of all along Gates Ave. near Hamburg Ave. But
difficulties were expected because many strikers and
their followers are living in this neighborhood, and
yesterday evening there were already disturbances there
when an attempt was made to run a repair car down the
tracks. The police said that it meant business.
Captain Kitzer has ordered his men to fire immediately,
and the Guard soldiers of the 7th Regiment which is
stationed nearby have the same order. Twelve sections
of wires were cut and the switches were blocked with
rocks.

Colonel Appleton (of the 7th Regiment) made the
following comment about the skirmish with the mob on the
evening before: I regret that the morning papers are
reporting that the volley was aimed over the heads of
the mob. That is absolutely wrong. We are not here to
fire into the air as a joke. Captain Palmer's people
had the order to shoot in order to kill or maim and it
was pure coincidence that no one in the mob was injured.
My men mean business.

At 8:15 a company of the 23rd Regiment marched to the ferry along 39th Street in order to meet 75 non-union people (scabs) and give them safe conduct up to the train station.

The men of the 23rd Regiment are bitterly complaining about the lack of nourishment since the little food they do get comes from friends and families.

Twenty scabs who had been fetched from Newark and Orange (New Jersey) put down their tools and joined the strikers.

The Executive Board of the Knights of Labor (i.e., the strike committee in Brooklyn) were ordered today to appear before the grand jury. They refused to testify.

The commissioner of arbitration, Feeney, held a long conference today with various high train officials. Afterwards he stated that the situation today was worse than it was eight days ago, and as far as he could see there was no hope for a settlement of the conflict.

January 23rd: The main difficulty with the Brooklyn strike today was the wires, many of which were cut last night. Everybody was anxious to see how Foreman Connelly (chairman of the strike committee) would act in regard to the linemen. Shortly after noon, Connelly announced that the linemen would strike. If the telephone or telegraph companies should try to send to the train companies their own people in order to repair the cut wires, then these, too, would go out on strike.

The lawless mobs cut even more wires last night so that the Fulton St. lines could not be run. . . . Wires were cut in Halsey St. and near Nostrand Ave. The big feed wire was severed so that no cars could run. The lines running from Flatbush Ave., Putnam Ave., Hulsey St., and Fulton St. to Tompkins Ave. and to East New York (a suburb of Brooklyn) were not running, and Fulton Street looked once again deserted. This was not the only case of wire cutting. In various unguarded parts of the city the strikers succeeded in paralyzing the companies. They cut the wires in Bergen St., Troy Ave., Ralph Ave., and Third Ave., and many other sections of wire were rendered unusable. In Marion St. a mob of people tore up the sidewalks last night and covered the tracks with stones.

Many of yesterday's events show clearly that the police sympathize with the strikers and that the men of the 2nd Brigade (Brooklyn Guard) do not like to oppose the mob. The only people who take their job seriously are the (Guard) soldiers of the City of New York who never hesitated to sweep the streets, if necessary at the point of their bayonets.

Many of the New York men have difficulties in obtaining the necessary rations. . . . The 12th Regiment is well located because the local people render it all kinds of assistance. . . . In other parts of the city

the regiments are being reviled and stoned, and they
have no great reserves of food. Therefore, the officers
and men in the restless districts are not in a very good
mood, and they will probably make use of their weapons
without hesitation as soon as they are asked to do so.

Henry Ahns, a sugar factory worker, died this
morning in the hospital. He was shot last night near
the stables at Haley St. and Broadway. He (Ahns) was
drunk at the time and did not stop when the sentry asked
him to.

In Ridgewood this morning, two street car lines
(Gates and Myrtle Ave.) were set in motion. Before this
action was taken, three companies of the 7th Regiment
that are stationed here broke up into small groups and
occupied the entire district (at Myrtle Ave. alone they
were stationed along an entire mile). A chain of
soldiers was formed all around two blocks of houses that
circle the street car coach-houses and nobody was
allowed inside who was not authorized. Along Gates Ave.
police stood at every corner. All gatherings of people
along the streets were dispersed; if two people stopped
in the street to talk to each other, they were told by
the police or the soldiers to move on. There was a lot
of activity in the depots . . . along the Myrtle Ave.
line, the first street car went by unmolested because
mounted police rode alongside of it. There were two
policemen in the front, and two in the back, of every
trolley car. Within five minutes other cars followed,
each one of them occupied by two policemen. Very few
passengers used the cars, but the train administration
was very encouraged by the success because the trains
had not been running for several days. The street car
officials wanted to put 30 cars into use today (usually
there are 48 trains that are running). They (the
officials) would like to put more into use, but they are
not needed and there are not enough policemen available
to protect them all.

In the course of the morning, the soldiers in the
vicinity of the coach-houses had the opportunity to fire
four shots. Several house owners refused to obey the
order to close their windows, so the soldiers fired
warning shots into the air. The open windows were
quickly closed.

Thirty cars, manned mostly by scabs from Jersey
City, were supposed to operate along Gates Ave. . . . .
Hardly had the first street car left when cut wires
stopped it cold.

The Brooklyn Heights Company announced that its
cars would run tonight until 10 p.m. Major Abrams of
the 7th Regiment, who commands the three companies at
Ridgewood, protested and declared that this entailed an
unnecessary risk since the street cars had no passengers
and the soldiers were tired from their long service and
in need of rest.

     The aforementioned Major Abrams closed all pubs in
the vicinity of Ridgewood at 8 p.m. He placed sentries
at the doors of every pub with the order to allow no one
in or out. A large number of people were actually kept
in captivity that way. Major Abrams stated that he
would probably close the pubs for an entire day. He
also closed the Assembly Hall in Ridgewood where the
strikers hold their meetings. There were three hundred
people in the hall at the time, who demanded
emphatically to be let out. Finally a messenger was
dispatched to look up the lawyer, Baldwin F. Strauss at
Fulton St., who appeared one hour later before Judge
Gaynor of the Supreme Court. Strauss demanded a writ of
habeus corpus that ordered Brigadier-General McLeer to
bring the locked-up workers before a court. The writ
was approved, but the lawyer of Brigadier-General McLeer
declared that he was insufficiently prepared and
demanded a postponement. Lawyer Strauss related the
details of the case and Judge Gaynor stated: 'I cannot
believe that the National Guard would be guilty of such
an act of lawlessness. If I could really believe it, I
would not approve a single minute of postponement. I
give you until 4 p.m. to reply to the accusations.'
     Towards 11 o'clock, two street cars (each filled
with 25 scabs) went down Third Avenue towards the
station on 58th Street. There were four policemen in
every car and two mounted policemen each in front and
behind it. Companies J and H of the 23rd Regiment were
lined up on both sides of the avenue between 24th and
58th Streets. Both cargos of scabs were delivered.
Crowds of strikers were pushing forward all along the
avenue, but they were dispersed by the two Guard
companies at the depot who chased them up the hill
behind 58th Street. The houses along the avenue were
ordered shut and bolted, and a series of apartment
buildings under construction between 56th and 57th
Streets had to be emptied of its workers upon the order
of the military. The piles of bricks, tiles and iron
located there was placed under guard. . . .
     A delegation of twelve citizens from Greenpoint (a
suburb of Brooklyn), who had been elected the evening
before at a mass meeting, appeared this morning before
Mayor Schieren and demanded that he should withdraw the
permit of the streetcars in their district so that the
streetcars would not keep running. The major referred
them to the city attorney. . . .
     January 24th: The main preoccupation of the mob in
Brooklyn last night seems to have been the destruction
of wires, because they destroyed more wires than at any
time since the beginning of the strike. Foreman
Connelly's order to strike was generally obeyed by the
linemen. . . .
     The 7th and 9th Avenue lines, which had been
running rather well yesterday, were totally paralyzed

today because of the destruction of trolley wires that
was carried out during the night by unknown persons
(probably strikers). There is very little chance that
the repairs will now be undertaken because all of the
linemen did not appear this morning. . . . Eight cars
from the train company, which stood only 200 feet from
the sheds and, at the most, a stone's throw from the
sentry lines, were so damaged that they were useless
without considerable repairs.

Various auxiliary policemen in Ridgewood took off
their insignia and resigned because it was too
cold. . . .

The roofer Thomas Carney, who had been shot (while
at work yesterday) by a National Guardsman at Harrison
St., died this morning at 3 o'clock in the hospital.
Colonel Austin of the 13th Regiment said today that he
has taken over the command of the regiment at Hicks St.
and that there will be no more shootings except under
dire circumstances. Instead of shootings, arrests will
be made.

This morning the switches at Troy Ave., Bergen St.
and Fulton St. were found to be covered with cement and
it took a long time to make them usable again.

Most of the soldiers (of the 7th Regiment New York)
are complaining about the cold last night as well as the
fact that the train companies are making no efforts
whatsoever to house them comfortably. The supply
section of the 7th Regiment's companies at Ridgewood is
located in the coach-sheds behind the boiler room where
a fire is maintained on the cement floor for cooking
purposes. Various National Guard soldiers who were
members of the high society (creme de la creme)
functioned as waiters, cooks, etc. A well-known artist
stood in front of a boiling pot, the secretary of an
insurance company was cooking plums, and a banker was
taking care of huge containers of steaming coffee. . . .
The Guard soldiers complained today about insufficient
rations, and they were promised more and better rations
for the afternoon. . . .

The president of a network of streetcars (Lewis)
declared that 300 street cars were in use--about 350
less than normal. At the moment, however, there would
be no reason for an increase because nobody is using the
trains. The night service would have to be carried out
at a loss for quite some time unless the traffic would
increase considerably. . . . They would have enough
people to man the street cars, but it would take some
time before the people would get used to their work
since they are strangers to the city. They must first
familiarize themselves with the streets along the lines
before they can be entrusted with a car, and that cannot
be done in an hour.

The elevated train companies are reaping great
profits. One of them reports a 107% increase in revenue

during this past week, and it has declared a magnanimous
10% bonus for its employees. The employees want to send
this bonus to the strikers.
January 25th: An exciting incident occurred this
morning at the Ridgeway station when about 25 new people
(scabs) arrived by elevated train. The strikers
immediately surrounded them and led them down Palmetto
Street before the police or Guard knew anything about
it. When the latter heard about it, a detachment of the
police and the Guard was dispatched in order to free the
scabs, and an exciting chase got underway while great
numbers of people were milling about the streets. The
Guard finally caught up with the kidnappers and their
captives, liberated 6 of them and returned them to the
sheds. The remaining 19 were brought to the
headquarters of the strikers and kept captive there.
A mass meeting of citizens will be held this
evening in Tivoli Hall at 8th Street near Third Avenue
in order to protest against the speed of the street cars
and against the inability of the train companies to put
a sufficient number of street cars at the disposal of
the public.
At 11:50 a trolley train of the Bashwick Ave. Line
reached the Maspeth border (a town which lies outside
the city limit). It was protected by two auxiliary
sheriffs and filled with about 20 scabs. The Maspeth
strikers, about 100 men, have their headquarters about a
quarter of a mile from the Grand Street Depot. As soon
as the trolley train arrived across from their
headquarters, it was taken by assault and the 20 scabs
were seized and carried into the hall. The two auxiliary
sheriffs were powerless. Two strikers took the trolley
train to the station and left it there. The train
officials immediately demanded a regiment to restore
peace.
January 26th: The wire cutting, which is the main
weapon of the strikers and their friends against the
Brooklyn trolley car companies, was continued last night
and this morning, and the train lines were hard hit
throughout the city. The wires were cut at fifteen to
twenty different places so that this morning there were
fewer trains running than is normal. . . .
The heavy snow and rain last night made life very
uncomfortable for the National Guard soldiers, and the
fog which subsequently covered the city did not improve
matters. . . . At 9 p.m. the fog was so thick that one
could not see ten feet ahead and the wires suffered
accordingly. The wire destroyers had an easy time since
they could carry out their task without being disturbed.
Not even their pals on the sidewalk were able to see
them.
During the last two days the wire wreckers have
shown that they know their business and very few wires
have actually been cut. Deflection of the electrical

current and the destruction of the wires by this process
was used in general. In some cases, wires were placed
across the trolley wires and then tied to iron posts
along the tracks. Within a few seconds the trolley wire
was burned up. Gas tubes were also used for this
purpose. One end of such a tube was placed on the
tracks while the other end was dropped on the trolley
wire which was burnt out within thirty seconds.
Attempts were also made to burn out the dynamos of the
power plants. . . .

Brigadier General McLeer said this morning that he
had not given any order to the National Guard to return
home and that he had no intention of doing so until all
disturbances had ceased, which was not yet the case.

The employees of the machine works will meet this
afternoon in order to consider whether they, too, should
not go on strike in support of the striking employees of
the trolley cars. . . .

The situation of the strikers is not bad, but the
decision of the judge to give the train companies three
weeks (20 days) to straighten out their difficulties
puts the workers to a hard test. The original demands
of the workers were: observance of the legal working
hours, better treatment for the substitute crews, a very
small raise in wages and a better work schedule. During
the most recent negotiations, the strikers dropped all
of their demands except for the observance of legal work
hours (10 hours) and the rehiring of the strikers. The
latter are very busy and successful in catching the
scabs, and the train companies are only able to run a
third of their cars. A bourgeois-Republican paper
estimates the cost of the strike until now at $717,250
of which $32,000 constitutes the loss of revenue of the
train companies. The train companies will make up for
their losses by paying less money to the new workers. A
general wage reduction of 50 cents a day will allow them
to wipe out their losses in a few months. The loss of
all the others (the workers, the state, etc.) is
irremediable.

The striking workers deserve unstinted praise for
their excellent discipline during the strike, a eulogy
which certainly must also be extended to the strike
leaders."

12

The Labor Protective Laws and the
Law-Abiding Citizens of Illinois/Socialism

In Illinois, the fight between the factory inspectorate and the employers over the enforcement of the Eight-Hour Law and the laws concerning women and children's work, continues. Mrs. Florence Kelley, the head of the Office of Factory Inspection, is now turning her attention to the big factories in the interior of the state and for this purpose recently traveled to Alton, Illinois, where there are important glass works which prosper splendidly through the work of children and long working hours. A bourgeois newspaper reports about this as follows:

Springfield, Illinois, January 12th: Mrs. Kelley, the Inspector of Factories for the state, recently inspected the Alton Glass Works at Alton and encountered numerous violations of the laws concerning the employment of minor children, violations of sanitary standards, and various other irregularities. She informed the owners and superintendents of the works of the results of her inspection and told them either to abide by the state laws or to close their factories. Mrs. Kelley returned to Springfield on Thursday and reported to the Governor (Altgeld) who immediately set up a meeting with the factory owners. Yesterday (January 11th) Senator C. A. Herb, editor J. J. McInerey and Mayor John J. Brenholt, all from Alton, and Edward Lewis, superintendent of the glass works, as well as the representatives (members of the legislature) Thomas Ferns and O. A. Snedecker from Jerseyville and P. McFee from Venine all appeared before the Governor to speak in favor of the accused. They admitted that the factories employed 700 boys, many of whom were under 14 years of age and who earned about 40

cents a day. The committee replied that many of
the children support poor parents and that they
have only the choice of working or starving. The
Governor then asked why, under these
circumstances, they were being paid such
ridiculously low wages. The superintendent
replied that the competition did not allow them to
pay higher wages. The Governor declared that the
violation of laws would no longer be tolerated.
The laws were to be carried out even if that would
mean that every plant and factory in the State of
Illinois would have to close. The law was
designed to protect the lives of children. He
gave the factory management until February 1st to
dismiss all children under the age of 12 and until
March 1st to dismiss all those under 14 years of
age.

Two days later, the following piece of news
appeared in the same paper:

"Alton, January 14th: Mrs. Kelley, the
Inspector of Factories returned today to this town
and gave final instruction on how to carry out the
laws concerning child labor in the Alton Glass
Works. In the evening she will travel to
Belleville for similar purposes. The affair has
been settled to the extent that all boys under 12
years of age will be dismissed by February 1st.
. . ."

Discussing the above-mentioned case and the
carrying out of the laws in general, Mrs. Kelley writes:

"This is the last of the companies that offers
open resistance. The big stockyards in Chicago all
have introduced the eight-hour day for their
10,000 employees, of which merely 926 are women
and children (to whom the law applies). All big
businessmen are either on bail because of legal
proceedings against them, or they have accepted
the eight-hour day. The Supreme Court still has
rendered no decision even though one was announced
for last July, and we will have carried out the
law in general (perhaps it will also be approved
of generally) before the decision by the Supreme
Court will be made. Many businessmen are already
saying that they will not re-introduce the long
work hours even if they are permitted to.
. . . "

Conditions such as exist in Alton would never have
occurred if the bourgeois authorities would have done
their duty. The office that should have been most

concerned, the Board of Education, did not do anything,
and the others--the mayor, senators and legislators--
demand the circumvention and open violation of the law.
And yet they call themselves law-abiding citizens!

* * * * *

The last presidential election (November 1894)
constituted a Waterloo for the Democratic Party. At the
same time, the Socialist Labor Party suffered heavy
losses in its bastions: New York and St. Louis. In New
York the loss of votes amounted to 20%. It was not very
much in St. Louis, but it was nevertheless remarkable
because of all the efforts that had been expended in the
preceding electoral campaign. The fact that the
Socialist Labor Party made considerable gains in other
states as, for example, New Jersey cannot hide the
unpleasant fact that it suffered, in part, significant
losses in its strongholds. But why?

The primary reason (although by no means the only
one) is the fact that the Socialist Labor Party has
dissipated and frittered away the electoral campaign
forces instead of gathering and concentrating them for
the assault of one specific point. It is all very nice
to sing: "My fatherland must be larger" and then to
extend one's arms and embrace all of mankind; but in
politics, singing and longing does not count--only
battling and calculating does. In politics, as well as
in mechanics, it is necessary to start out at first from
a firm point from which all forces must be set into
motion in order to conquer new territories. In the
resolutions concerning the position of the International
Workingman's Association which was passed by the
congress at Philadelphia on April 12th, 1874, we read
among other items:

"The Federation (the International) should
only become involved in an actual electoral
campaign when it has become strong enough to
exercise noticeable influence and then only upon
the basis of the community (commune) from which
the electoral movement may spread to the larger
community (counties, states, United States), all
depending on the circumstances and in harmony with
the resolutions of the congress. . . . "

The Unity Congress of the Labor Party of the United
States decided on July 21st, 1876 to appeal to the party
sections and to the workers in general:

"to abstain for the time being (it was a
presidential election year) from any
electioneering and to turn one's back to the
ballot box . . . Let us wait for our turn! And

our turn will come! . . . "

And among the reasons for its opinions, we find the following:

"Considering that the ballot box of this country has long ceased to represent the people's will and has fallen into the hands of professional politicians who use it to falsify the people's will,
Considering that the bourgeois republic produces an infinite number of petit-bourgeois reformers and quacks whose penetration of the Labor Party is facilitated by our participation in the electoral process,
Considering further that the corruption of the ballot box and the games at reform reach their zenith during presidential election years (and general elections as a rule), it is clear that they represent the greatest danger for the Labor Party."

The resolutions and considerations seem as timely today as they were twenty years ago, and these considerations and resolutions also contain the nucleus for a policy that ought to be used if the Socialist Labor Party wants to achieve successes that stand in true relationship to the efforts that have been expended. It is certain, by the way, that other local reasons contributed to the lack of success.
In a former report it was stated that "even the socialists in the various western towns are making common cause with the Populists." Chicago stands out, and the situation there is described by an experienced worker who stands right in the midst of it., He sent the following interesting report dated December 23rd, 1894:
" . . . We live in a time of ferment and it seems to me that a Socialist party is in the process of taking shape. At least, in Chicago one gets that impression. In this connection, the People's Party-Populist movement is very instructive. Originally a few boodle politicians' decided to fish in troubled water by exploiting the general dissatisfaction of the workers with the political parties. They called together a convention at Springfield, Illinois. There, a program was to be adopted that any politician could subscribe to. Then the Democrats were to be supported--but not all of them. The main idea was to help Mayor Hopkins and his friends. The whole plan, however, fell through because of the participation of honest union members, particularly of Socialists. At Springfield, a program was adopted which, even though it contained contradictory and hardly acceptable demands, was

nevertheless constituted in such a way that it could be
used to preach socialism. And that is exactly what the
Socialists intended to do when they joined the People's
Party. It is actually wrong to use the word "join"
here, because the Socialists were given as many
representatives at the Chicago convention as the
Populists. Besides, the third group--which consisted of
trade unionists, Turnvereine and several other leagues--
sent many Socialists. The single tax people were
numerically weak and they were only important because
they are supported everywhere (also in Denver) by the
boodle elements, who are compelled to appear radical but
cannot support the Socialists who do not want to have
anything to do with them. The Pomeroys[2] and similar
demagogues are being pushed forward by the masses.
There is no place for them in a Socialist party, so they
carry on all sorts of affairs on the side; and for those
affairs, Henry George is just the right man. The local
political movement is thus not a genuine populist
movement. The Socialists stood in the forefront during
the election campaign. Strict defenders of the People's
Party also spoke, but they were usually outsiders. The
alliance is by no means a firm one, but as Henry D.
Lloyd has written in a letter to the (German)
"Typographia" Nr. 9, it is a loose one which will hardly
last because Socialist and petit-bourgeois elements
cannot work together in the long run.
     You must have heard of Henry D. Lloyd. He is an
American writer. For ten years, he was the financial
director of the local "Tribune," one of the largest
capitalist (Republican) newspapers in the country. He
is independent because he is very rich. The local
papers consider him a millionaire. He has been
transformed from a philanthropist into a Socialist. His
newest work is entitled "Wealth against Commonwealth"
and is published by Harper Brothers. It deals with the
trusts, particularly the oil trusts (Standard Oil
Company). It is based on official sources. Lloyd makes
use of the last two chapters to give his own views.
     The movement has shown that there is a whole group
of educated men who are Socialists or who are in the
process of becoming so. There is Clarence B. Darrow,
one of the most prominent attorneys of the city, who is
highly respected by the Democrats and was seriously
considered by them as a candidate for the Senate. He
dissociated himself from the Democrats and also attacked
the Republicans fiercely during a speech to a large
assembly in the Auditorium[3] (all five thousand seats
were taken). He declared himself in favor of the
Populist Party but it was a strange declaration. He
ignored the entire program of the Populist Party,
declaring that it did not really matter what it
contained. He said that what is important is not what
is written on paper but that which lives in the heart of

the people and contributes to the development of
industry; and he went on to express very poetically what
Marx talks about very graphically in the seventh part of
the twenty-fourth chapter of the first volume. I was
extremely, if pleasantly, surprised because I had
believed that he belonged to the Tucker Anarchists.[4]
Instead, he spoke like a convinced Marxist. I must have
Trumbull's speech and I will send it to you. Even if one
cannot call it Socialist, it is nevertheless extremely
interesting.

    There is no doubt that the whole movement here has
helped Socialism, because Socialist speakers criticized
the Populist program and in front of many thousands of
people. At the moment, only the Socialist clubs seem to
exist. What will happen in the spring is hard to tell
at this time. You know how dispersed the entire local
movement is. We have here Tucker Anarchists, Peukert
Anarchists, Most Anarchists, Social Democrats of New
York or Cincinnati persuasion (furthermore, Socialists
of no particular persuasion (like myself) and trade
unionists with Socialist leanings. Actually, all of
these tendencies are not as much separated from each
other as their enumeration may imply. Often there is a
wild intermingling. No faction has succeeded in
absorbing another even though they all cooperate during
the electoral campaigns and belong to the same leagues.
There are only a few Tuckerians, and they lack any kind
of organization. The organizations of the Social
Democrats of all shades number perhaps 250 members.
Peukert has the Debate Club behind him in which many
different tendencies are included. The club has perhaps
from 30 to 50 members. In general, it remains quiet.
He is also the cock of the roost in the Union of German
Painters (house painters). The painters have about 250
members. The two or three different Most groups have
hardly 50 to 60 members. The corporation which
published the Arbeiterzeitung contains all sorts of
Socialist views which are reflected in the paper.
Before I forget it, the Populist Party of Illinois has
only gained followers among the industrial workers, and
it has actually lost adherents among the farmers. The
Populist Party got 25,000 votes in Chicago (1500 during
the last elections) and 25,000 in the country. Since
all of the coal miners and many rural industrial workers
supported the Populists, and since the total number of
votes in Illinois (during the past elections) amounted
to 24,000, it is apparent that what I said above is
true. In Illinois, the majority of those who vote
Populist are industrial workers. If the party should
continue, this circumstance will make itself felt. In
order to evaluate all of these party configurations, one
has to think of the beginnings of the Socialist Party in
Germany. The move is on to bring the German Socialists
here closer together. If it should bear fruit, then the

next task would be to spread Socialist literature in the
English language. What is needed here is a concerted
action. As far as free silver is concerned, there is
not much enthusiasm for it among the workers despite all
of the noise emitted mainly by the refugees (because of
the panic) from the silver states. During the electoral
campaign, there was little talk about free silver but
all the more talk of the cooperative commonwealth and
Plank 10."

The New York Socialists have been placed into a
very bad position since the convention of the American
Federation of Labor (1890) at Detroit. The rejection of
the delegates of the Central Labor Federation (of New
York) has filled them with such wrath, that out of
opposition to the AFL--or better, its leaders--they let
themselves be carried away to do things that harmed not
only them but the cause they stand for. Here are a few
examples:

When in 1893 delegations of French workers traveled
to Chicago in order to attend the World Fair, they were
given receptions in New York by both the Central Labor
Union and the Central Labor Federation. Both
organizations used these occasions to launch attacks
upon each other in order to force the French workers to
take sides, which put the foreign guests into an
embarrassing situation.

When John Burns arrived here at the beginning of
last December, the Socialists launched a fierce attack
upon him in their English language newspaper. When he
went on to Denver, the same newspaper published a letter
from the Social Democratic Federation of London which
was designed to follow him out west like a warrant.
These people did not seem to know that John Burns, as
representative of British labor, was traveling to the
convention of the AFL at Denver in his capacity of
delegate of the Parliamentary Committee of the British
unions.

When Gompers was defeated during the election to
the presidency of the American Federation of Labor at
Denver, the New York Socialists held a victory
celebration, without realizing that they were thus also
celebrating the end of Plank 10, the removal of the
headquarters of the American Federation of Labor into
the interior of the country, and the election of John
McBride.

Public demonstrations and incidents of such a
nature might arouse attention in our sensation-hungry
era; they will certainly fail to arouse sympathy. It
was correctly observed that such happenings are not
illustrative of a lack of tactics, but a lack of tact.
Years of continuous attacks upon a single person must be
judged similarly.

For several years now, the German Socialists have
begun in many towns to found schools (preferably taught

in German) for their children, to give them help (on
Saturdays and Sundays) in subjects which are either
neglected or not taught at all in the public schools.
If the success of these schools is not always the
greatest, it must not in all circumstances be blamed on
the directors of these institutions but rather on the
local circumstances. Nevertheless, these schools lack a
uniform direction, a uniform curriculum and uniform
educational materials. Without these prerequisites, the
whole matter will be left to chance or even the caprices
of individuals, and these schools will have no future.
Adult educational schools (especially to teach English)
have been set up in several towns. The Socialists have
also furnished inns and pubs for the party comrades
which have not worked out very well. The best known
place of this type (it combines school, assembly place
and pub) is the Labor Lyceum in Brooklyn (New York),
whose plot of land and main building were given twelve
years ago as a present for educational and other
purposes to the Social Democratic Labor Party by an old
party comrade, Dr. F. Gerau.

Chapter XII: Endnotes

[1]Boodle is the name for corruption or bribe funds.
Boodle politicians are politicians that accept bribes or
hand them out.

[2]An American labor leader in Chicago who has great
oratorical ability.

13
The Labor Movement in 1895

The budget of the labor movement in the United States for the year 1895 shows a considerable deficit.

The year began with the great strike of the employees of the trolley cars in Brooklyn, New York, and ended with the strike of employees of the same category in Philadelphia, where in mid-December 6,000 people stopped working in order to protect themselves against attacks upon their organization. The battle in Philadelphia was much shorter than the one in Brooklyn, but the result was the same: defeat here as well as there since not a single demand of the workers was accepted. The result must be chiefly ascribed to the lack of experience that prevails among the ranks of the trolley employees. The employees of the electric trains are primarily recruited from younger people that have enjoyed an average education but who have not learned any productive trade so that they cannot find jobs in the overcrowded business world or even as clerks. Having originated from petit-bourgeois circles and having been filled with petit-bourgeois ideas, they enter the fray easily, but they are just as easily caught and cheated by the saccharine phrases of the philanthropists and the hypocritical speeches of the political careerists. Thus it happened with the strikers of Philadelphia who even took as their attorney the former Postmaster-General, John Wanamaker, the owner of Philadelphia'a world-famous department store.

Unemployment and reduction of wages placed heavy burdens on the working class during the years 1893 and 1894. The brutal suppression of the Pullman Strike and the subsequent massive disciplinary measures have created widespread discouragement, and the larger organizations must use all of their strength to remain afloat. They avoided, therefore, any large conflict

during the past year, with the exception of the coal
miners of Western Pennsylvania and the ready-made
clothes tailors of New York who were able to make small
gains after short strike actions. Business revived
somewhat after the approval of the new tariff law and
there was a very moderate upswing in industry so that
workers were recalled, and here and there was a small
improvement of their wages that had fallen
precipitously. Even Frick, the sad hero of Homestead,
found it necessary to give a small raise to the coke
workers whose situation and battles have often been
reported by the Neue Zeit. The bourgeois press took
ostentatious notice of such occurrences and even though
the workers had themselves experienced the hollowness of
the beautiful phrases of renewed industrial activity,
they were too weak to make any special efforts to
improve their situation. This becomes most evident if
one examines the situation and the activity (or lack of
activity) of the country's large unions.

The American Railway Union, the union of railroad
employees, seems to have good people because it was not
destroyed by the defeat of July 1894 and it is beginning
everywhere, especially in the South and West, to
strengthen and complete its organization. It even seems
that it is getting ready for new battles even though it
is avoiding all provocations. E. V. Debs, the courageous
and skillful president of the organization, who was
recently released from prison where he had spent six
months for allegedly disregarding a court injunction,
has once again resumed his work for the American Railway
Union. For the time being, he is giving lectures in all
of the larger cities of the Midwest and West of the
country, during which he emphasizes that a permanent
improvement of conditions can only be achieved by the
permanent use of the right to vote. By the permanent
use of the vote he means, for the time being, adherence
to the "Populists"--the movement of the small farmers.

The Order of the Knights of Labor, whose decline
has been observed for over a year, is even more strongly
tied to the Populists, even though this has not
prevented the extinction of its splendor. The current
Grand Master Workman, Sovereign, was even so childishly
naive as to call for a boycott in late summer against
the widely circulating, well-secured notes of the
national banks and to proclaim that this would help the
Populists in their efforts to spoil and debase the
currency. The boycott was completely ignored. The
beautiful headquarters of the order, which had been
built at a great cost in Philadelphia, was sold and the
order's chancellery has been moved to Washington, the
seat of the government of the United States. In mid-
November the annual General Assembly of the Order took
place in Washington where it became apparent just how
much the Order had declined. As is common during such

circumstances, bitter quarrels broke out particularly
with the Socialists, about which we will have more to
say. Besides the latter, the former long-term Grand
Master Workman, Powderly, works with all his might
against the survival of the order, which does indeed
seem rather endangered.
     The American Federation of Labor held its annual
convention from December 9th until the 17th in New York
where 96 delegates represented about 250,000 union
members whereas during the previous year (1894) in
Denver, 77 delegates represented about the same number
of workers. The greater number of delegates may be
explained by the fact that New York has greater powers
of attraction and also more organizations than the West.
The impact of the bad times is evident from the number
of votes of each delegate (1 vote for each 100 members):

Delegates of the Barbers	1894:	17 votes
	1895:	only 15
Delegates of the Bakers	1894:	50 votes
	1895:	only 40
Delegates of the Brass Workers	1894:	10 votes
	1895:	only 5
Delegates of the Waiters, etc.	1894:	20 votes
	1895:	only 16
Delegates of the Iron Workers	1894:	156 votes
	1895:	only 120
Delegates of the Coal Miners	1894:	345 votes
	1895:	only 181
Delegates of the Painters	1894:	80 votes
	1895:	only 51
Delegates of the Carpenters	1894:	8 votes
	1895:	only 7
Delegates of the Streetcar Employees	1894:	40 votes
	1895:	only 25
Delegates of the Tailors (Custom)	1894:	50 votes
	1895:	only 42
Delegates of the Typographers	1894:	80 votes
	1895:	only 73

     On the other hand, the cobblers had 41 at Denver
but 100 at New York, and the Ready-Made Clothes' Tailors
had 100 in Denver but 122 in New York.
     Of the unions which were represented at Denver
(1894), the following were missing at New York: the
wheelwrights, the glassworkers, the shoe workers, the
clerks and the tin and sheet metal workers. On the
other hand, there were present in New York but not
present at Denver: the sales' agents, the furriers, the
granite stone masons, the International Machinists'
Union, the potters, the printers (in contrast to the
compositors-typographers), the spinners, actors, dyers
and bleachers, the blast furnace workers, the butchers,
the diamond workers, the fishermen and the stokers and

firemen on steamers, etc.

In his message to the Convention, President McBride reported that the Federation's organ "The Federationist" is in good shape and that the federation is numerically and financially stronger (?) than in 1894. He also reported that many small strikes had a positive ending and that the more important ones, those of the ready-made clothes' tailors and coal miners resulted in some advantages. He recommended that the powers of the federal and state central bodies (central labor union, etc.) should be more closely defined, that certain constitutional obstacles to labor legislation should be removed and that the Federation, for the time being, should try to obtain a law regarding patents as well as a law against the arbitrary and autocratic handling of court injunctions. He declared that the augmentation of the federal debt by gold loans is the greatest crime of the century and that further efforts must be made to reduce working hours. He called for the workers' involvement in politics, albeit not within their own independent political party, and he espoused the recognition of the Cuban insurgents as a belligerent force. He welcomed the delegates of the British Trade Union Congress and reported without further recommendation, in a purely businesslike way, that the Federation had been invited to send delegates to the International Congress which meets in London in August of 1896.

The receipts of the Federation amounted to $18,943 whereas the expenditures were $15,612. The year before, the receipts were $22,493 and the expenditures $17,302.

The expenditures for the Federation's organ, "The Federationist," amounted to $2,675 whereas the receipts were $3,184. It should be noted that the receipts from subscriptions amounted to only $320 but advertising brought in $2,864. Among expenditures is included the sum of $870 for compensation and interest payments to advertising agents (these sums do not include cents and fractions).

The secretary of the Federation also gave a long report. He complained about the many unnecessary expenditures and consoled the advocates of newer methods by expressing the hope that future generations might adopt these. He demanded the abolition of patent laws in order to make new inventions and machines available to everyone, etc.

The convention issued resolutions against the death penalty, the limitation of voting rights through educational criteria, and against the compulsory mediation laws which are before congress. Other resolutions spoke in favor of the nationalization of the telegraph system and the use of initiative and referendum. The expenditure of $500 was approved in order to organize the textile workers in the Southern

states, and it was decided to make new efforts to
achieve the eight-hour day. The National Brewers' Union
was given the alternative of breaking their ties to the
Knights of Labor or to have to relinquish all further
support and recognition by the Federation. Several
boycotts were lifted but others were initiated even
though a delegate (and official of the Federation)
reported that there were 233 boycotts this year which
met with little support. Cincinnati was selected as the
site of the next convention, and McBride and A. Strasser
were elected as delegates to the next British Trade
Union Congress. The following decisions merit special
mentioning: a) Support for free silver coinage in a
ratio of 16:1; b) Rejection of any political program for
the Federation; c) Approval of the Federation's
participation at the International Congress in London in
1896. The convention then took up the agenda. On
several occasions the Convention displayed great
irritability towards the Socialists, particularly those
from New York. The main interest of the convention
focused on the electoral battle between McBride and S.
Gompers. S. Gompers was elected president for the
coming year by 1041 votes, whereas McBride received only
1023 votes.
     The fragmentation of the proletarians' ranks in New
York and environs which is regrettable just by itself,
which makes itself felt in all of the political and
economic battles of the workers and which is
demonstrated by the existence of large numbers of
central bodies that fight each other, has increased even
more this year. Patterning itself after the New York
Central Labor Federation, of which we have often
reported, there has been for quite some time a Socialist
Labor Federation in Brooklyn, the sister city of New
York, a Central Labor Federation in Newark, New Jersey
and in a similar way, the United Jewish Trade Unions in
New York. All of these groups maintain clear socialist
principles and stand in open or hidden conflict with the
older, pure and simple labor union councils of the
above-mentioned towns. The labor unions of these
Socialist associations and the associations themselves
(except for the above-mentioned United Jewish Unions) do
not have many members but they make up for it by being
all the more active. They are, indeed, the self-
sacrificing auxiliary troops of the Socialist Labor
Party. Many of the leaders of the latter, particularly
those whose economic and class position did not allow
them to join a union, have belonged for quite some time
to the order of the Knights of Labor who, as is well
known, accept everyone except publicans, bankers and
lawyers. For years, these Socialist Knights of Labor
have launched sharp and justified attacks upon the
former Grand Master Workman, Powderly, and they
contributed to his downfall. It seems that at the

penultimate General Assembly of the Order (1894) certain
agreements were concluded between the officials of the
Order and the Socialists according to which a member of
the latter was to take over the editorship of the organ
of the Knights of Labor, "Journal of the Knights of
Labor," during the following year (1895) as a reward for
services rendered or as recognition for outstanding
abilities. In the meantime, the new year of publication
began and no Socialists were employed because the means
were lacking to pay decent salaries according to the
officials of the Order. This interlude, as well as the
intense activity on behalf of the Populists by the
current Grand Master Workman, Sovereign, and the silly
boycott of the notes of the national banks, considerably
increased the dissatisfaction of the Socialist Knights
of Labor; and when, as a final straw, they were accused
of the non-observance of a boycott, they rose in
rebellion and opened up the fight against the executive
board of the Order--in the press as well as at the
annual General Assembly. The Order suffered losses, and
the once highly influential and highly respected
District Assembly 49 of New York City was seriously
weakened.

During the last state-wide elections in November
1895, the Socialist Labor Party made up for the previous
year and its members regained their confidence. A
liaison with the adjacent Socialist labor union groups
of New York, Brooklyn, Newark and other towns had long
been planned and partially realized. The Socialist
Knights of Labor urged new undertakings and made all the
necessary preparations for them. They made use of the
occasion of the annual Convention of the American
Federation of Labor in December of last year, in order
to hold a large assembly where they founded a new
central organization and proclaimed the Socialist Trade
and Labor Alliance of the United States and Canada.

The new organization was as much directed against
the Knights of Labor as against the American Federation
of Labor. Thus it does not lack opposition from the
outside, an opposition which is, however, almost
surpassed by internal schism. An old party comrade, who
is highly respected within the Socialist Labor Party,
after first giving a long report about the founding and
the principles of the new organization, writes as
follows: "What is the alliance supposed to become? An
organization for Socialist propaganda or a substantial
labor union battle organization which will be a rival to
the already existing two central bodies of this land?
In the first case, the new organization, to be sure,
would lead a rather harmless existence which would be,
however, of little use to the Socialist Labor Party. It
would encroach upon its business and then simply become
superfluous. In the latter case, however, it is clear
that my party comrades, the Socialists, have assumed a

frightening responsibility if, by founding this
undertaking, they create new occasions to pour oil into
the fire of fratricidal strife within the ranks of
organized labor!"

During the last few days of the year, a well-
attended convention of Jewish Socialists took place at
New York. Delegates from a great number of Jewish labor
unions and leagues, for the most part from New York and
environs but also from Boston, New Haven, Philadelphia,
Newark and other towns, consulted about taking common
action. Some arrived from the more remote parts of the
country such as Chicago, San Francisco and other towns.
These Jewish Socialists form a respectable auxiliary
force of the Socialist Labor Party, and they already
possess several newspapers in Yiddish. The regulation of
the administration and the editorship of these papers
formed the main topic of the consultations. The slogan
of the participants was characteristic: "We are not
Jewish, but Jewish-speaking workers and Socialists."

It has often been mentioned in former reports that
about the same fragmentation mania that exists among the
workers of New York and other towns also prevails in
Chicago. Two events during the past year aroused no
little interest: The founding of a new central body
called the "Labor Congress" and the firing and
resignation of several editors of the Chicago
Arbeiterzeitung. An experienced man writes from there
about the founding of the new central body:

> "The 'Labor Congress' was founded by
> Socialist trade unionists who had become
> dissatisfied with the corrupt practices of the old
> politicians of the Trade and Labor Assembly. The
> word "Socialist" here must be interpreted in its
> widest sense. The left wing of the Populist Party
> is regarded here, too, as Socialist. The
> strongest contingent is supplied by the various
> units of the Cigar Makers' Union. Furthermore,
> the German and Bohemian Central Labor Union, the
> farriers, the tailors, the German book printers,
> etc., belong to it. The majority of the delegates
> are Germans, but a considerable number of the
> leaders are Americans or totally Americanized
> foreigners (people who immigrated at a young age).
> Some of the most outstanding leaders are members
> of the Socialist Labor Party. In order to
> overcome the drawback that so many non-workers
> happened to be delegates to the Trade and Labor
> Assembly, it was ruled that only a worker (in a
> factory) can be a delegate. As a result, the
> founder of the Labor Congress himself had to
> resign because of his own rule. . . . "

The same person writes about the occurrences at the
Arbeiterzeitung of Chicago:

"Differences of opinion between the editors
and the directors led to the dismissal of the
editor-in-chief, whereupon two other editors
voluntarily resigned. The alleged reason: people
like Henry Santos, etc., had not been praised
sufficiently. Since there is an endless number of
cliques at Chicago, other factors played an
additional, if minor, role. All of this was
discussed, but the real reason was not touched
upon. The real reason was the refusal of the
editorial board to take care of the private
business of the directors. They also failed to
show the expected reverence towards the directors.
But let us not forget about the newspaper because
of this. An opposition has been formed which will
attack the enemy's most vulnerable spot: the
elections to directorship. The majority of the
shareholders are not even happy with this type of
editorship, but they know enough to realize that
the main weapon of the proletariat here must not
be destroyed just because it finds itself in the
wrong hands for the time being. Why, however,
does the paper find itself today, even if
temporarily, in the hands of private people? (Not
theoretically, but practically). The main reason
is the inability of the Socialist Labor Party of
America to find the right tactics. When the
Arbeiterzeitung Corporation was organized, there
were a number of Social Democrats among its
organizers. They were in the minority and it may
well be that this minority was artificially
created. But instead of making use of this defeat
in order to prepare for future victories, they
capitulated and left the paper to their enemies.
A few of them, however, remained at their posts
and it is due to them alone that the Socialist
Labor Party was at least occasionally treated in a
fair manner. The characterization which the Neue
Zeit used for the Socialist Labor Party could also
be applied to Chicago. If it were not applicable
to Chicago, the Arbeiterzeitung would look
different than it is today.
     Nothing is more suitable to produce
pessimists than to render exaggerated descriptions
of the progress of the Socialists and to blow up
small successes. The boomerang never fails to
appear. The agitation of the Germans is often
forced because it is not based on facts. It is no
coincidence that of the many Socialists that have
immigrated, only a few belong to Socialist
organizations and some of them have even joined

the old parties. Yes, there are even people who do not subscribe to a single Socialist paper but who consider themselves Socialists. I believe that the explanation for all of this is very simple. It is still possible for a relatively large number of people to obtain savings. There are whole streets of workers (in Chicago) that belong to workers, and I personally know of workers who have become the owners of several houses within the span of ten to fifteen years. If a worker believes that he can work himself up as an individual, then his interests change and, as a rule, he is lost to the movement. As the owner of a small house, he becomes interested only in immediate, small-time reforms. The pavement of streets, the building of canals, taxes and similar items sometimes become vital matters to him. Since his property has (practically) made him a petit-bourgeois, he soon becomes one theoretically. The Socialist becomes a follower of the old parties as soon as the proletarian is transformed into a petit-bourgeois. The concepts of factory worker and petit-bourgeois are not mutually exclusive. For the careful observer, however, it becomes apparent that the petit-bourgeois splendor, if there ever was one, has passed its apogee and it would vanish even more rapidly were it not for the work done by minors. I know of families which are chiefly saved from perdition by its youthful members. Therefore, also, the equanimity with which the workers of Illinois view the abolition or enforcement of labor protection laws. But in spite of everything, one can detect the beginnings of improvement. It is true that the local Socialist organizations are in very sad shape and that the conditions in Chicago are horrendous. But I am convinced that this, too, will change with time.

One of the editors of the Arbeiterzeitung who had resigned was elected by a great majority into the directory (administrative board) of the same paper and even though he finds himself there for the moment in a hopeless minority, it will be a different story in one or two years. The Arbeiterzeitung will then become once more a fighting organ of the Socialists. Time, patience and work can achieve miracles. . . .

Even though the Socialist organizations find themselves in such a miserable situation, the Socialist ideas have nevertheless struck deeper roots in the American people, which I noticed when I came in touch with many agents and urban travelers. . . .

What has happened to freedom of speech here
is illustrated by the fact that the Englishman
Mowbray was interrupted by a police captain during
an assembly. At another gathering, he received
the following instruction from the captain of the
police: 'The police will not be criticized'!
This is how far we have come in Chicago. And what
are the English-speaking workers of the Trade and
Labor Assembly up to? Their leaders want to
organize a regiment for--Cuba!"

In Milwaukee, Cincinnati, Cleveland, San Francisco
and other towns, the situation is similar to that in New
York and Chicago.
The working class of the United States did not
arouse any respect among the economic and political
rulers during this past year. The quarrels among the
different unions, the necessary efforts of the
organizations to maintain their existence, to regain
lost ground and to obtain work and bread, the hollow
eulogies of petit-bourgeois plans and reforms--all of
this contributed to paralyze the forces of the American
proletariat so that all aggressively pursued policy
vanished during 1895. The exploiting class was the
tertius gaudens and acted accordingly by capturing or
damaging important positions of the working class and by
even adding insult to injury.
I have previously reported about the domestic
policy of the State and the City of New York. In 1893
the Republican Party obtained the majority in the
legislature of the state and formed the so-called Lexow
Committee to investigate the conditions in the City of
New York, particularly in the police department. The
revelations concerning the corruption therein served to
discredit the infamous Tammany Hall, which in 1894 was
defeated for the first time in many years by a
combination of the Republican Party, "respectable
citizens" and a diverse coterie of dissatisfied people
among which the German and Jewish workers formed a
strong contingent. The administration of the city was
placed into "honest" hands and the legislature of the
state did everything possible to help the new mayor to
clean the Augean stables by empowering him to fire
within six months all heads of departments, police
judges, etc., and to fill the vacant positions with new
people. The citizenry cheered, the mayor carried out
the desired firings and hirings, and the result was that
budget and taxes rose, the police subjected the
inhabitants to miserable chicaneries, and the workers
and their organizations were disregarded and mocked.
Robust and dashing military officers received the most
important positions in the police commission and the
highway department, and the chief of the latter, a
former colonel, snubbed the labor organizations who had

lodged a complaint with him and insulted them by calling
them idlers and similar terms. The discovery of
violators against the Sunday Law became the chief task
of the police, and their promotions depended upon their
eagerness and energy to proceed against strikers.
During the examination which was given to the police
inspectors that were competing for the position of chief
of police, the most important and decisive questions
dealt with their possible actions during strikes and the
unlawful assembly that might result from them. The
answer of one candidate, that he would concentrate his
units at certain points of the city and set up guns
which would spit out grenades and shrapnel, satisfied
the police commission to such an extent that it secured
for that man the desired position of chief of police of
New York City.

The stubborn attempts of the new police commission
to strictly enforce the Sunday Law enabled Tammany Hall
last November (1895) to win a renewed victory in the
City of New York, with which it can do, however, very
little for the time being. The rude tone which reform
officials and policemen have been using against the
workers has resulted in the return of the apostates to
the Socialist Labor Party. They not only made up for
the loss of 1894 but were able to register an increase
of votes.

The Republican legislators, who had come into power
unexpectedly in the states of New York and New Jersey,
went so far in their eagerness to reform that they
launched sharp attacks upon the Statistical Labor Office
and the Institute of Factory Inspection. In New Jersey,
a committee of the legislature suggested that the
Institution should be totally abolished since the
federal government's department would suffice. In the
meantime, the gentlemen people's representatives limit
themselves to personnel changes, i.e., they fill the
offices with members of their own party. They will keep
quiet during 1894 which is a presidential election year.

It has been pointed out earlier that the different
labor protection laws that have been wrested from the
legislatures, are in the end usually either annulled or
rendered ineffective by the courts of this country.
This happened, for instance, to the laws dealing with
the truck system, the Employers' Liability Act, the laws
reducing working hours and other similar ones. Judicial
power and respect are untouchable objects of veneration
for the Anglo-American populace, and the American judges
have fully earned this veneration and esteem from the
bourgeois possessing class by their painstaking
upholding of the Manchester principles and their
intervention in the actions of the workers. The Pullman
Strike of 1894 is still in everybody's memory and was by
far the greatest achievement of judicial bias in favor
of the exploiting society. A new strike against the

labor protective legislation was carried out last spring. As has been reported before, the legislature of the State of Illinois, three years ago issued a law for the protection of children, minors and women, declaring that eight hours constitute the maximum allowable work hours for them. It also established a factory inspectorate in order to enforce these laws. The factory inspectors under the leadership of Mrs. Florence Kelley eagerly went to work, hauled the violators of this law before the court and achieved great successes until the factory owners attacked the constitutionality of the law and appealed to the supreme court of the state; last March, it declared the aforementioned law as unconstitutional since it limited the freedom of contract of adults (women). In order to maintain a semblance of philanthropy, the court declared moreover: "We do not want to be understood as to be declaring the unconstitutionality of Section 5 (of the law) if the stipulations are limited to minors of the female sex." This decision has robbed the law of its teeth, even though the factory inspectors continue their activities on behalf of the children and against the system of sweat shops.

In one of the worst districts of Chicago, the "East End" of the city, philanthropic ladies have founded the Hull House in order to render philanthropic services to the very poor population of that part of the city which consists mostly of Southern European immigrants. These same ladies, who belong to influential circles and families, contributed much towards the issuance and enforcement of the aforementioned law. The mightiest foe and vanquisher of the Eight Hour Law, the Manufacturers Association of Illinois, offered this institution and these women $50,000 if they would stop their agitation on behalf of this law. The offer was refused.

The Supreme Court of the United States delivered a little masterpiece of judicial arrogance by declaring a law of the Congress of the United States as illegal, an event that until now has rarely happened because the judges are dependent upon the good will of the Congress for their salaries, assistance, equipment of the courts, etc., and Congress is in no hurry to agree to the requests and demands of the Justice Department because there is little patronage to be had there. When the new (Wilson) Tariff Law passed (a moderate ten to fifteen per cent lowering of the McKinley Tariff Law) a small income tax was passed simultaneously in order to create an equilibrium as far as the revenues were concerned, whereupon those who were touched by it raised immediate protests. Legal proceedings were undertaken which produced the result that the Supreme Court of the United States, on May 20th, declared the income tax to be unconstitutional because it did not apply to all people

to the same degree, etc. The decision passed, five to
four. The poor threatened millionaires described the
income tax as a socialist measure. The judges which had
rendered the minority opinion, on the other hand,
accused the majority of the Supreme Court of having
forged a weapon that opens a path for Socialism.

These examples, as well as many others which have
been mentioned earlier, point to the difficulties with
which the working class of the United States has to
contend in order to obtain even the most modest labor
protection laws, and they also show the obstacles which
it has to overcome in order to have these laws put into
action. But the fact that the American bourgeoisie,
despite it all, does not feel secure, is illustrated by
its all-out preparations to defend and maintain its
privileges, the spending of large sums of money in
various states for the construction of armories and
fortresses, and the silent but steady purges in National
Guard regiments of suspected soldiers. The same
phenomenon is illustrated by the constantly increasing
demands of the upper bourgeoisie, the professional
soldiers and their lackeys in Congress for a significant
increase of the professional army (now only 25,000 men)
and the concentration of federal troops near the large
cities and industrial centers. The same motives
underlie to a large extent the recently erupted
chauvinism ("jingoism") in Congress and the bourgeois
press of the country, which indubitably serves to
alienate the working class from its emancipatory
aspirations and to anaesthetize it with patriotic
phrases. What Napoleon III, Bismarck and others
accomplished in this field across the ocean may also be
achieved by the bourgeoisie of the United States if the
fragmentation of the forces of organized labor is not
brought to a halt. And the American bourgeoisie
certainly does not lack the means, the material means,
to give it a good try. It knew and it knows how to make
use of its gigantic area of exploitation. The motto:
"A human being does not come into his own until he has
become a baron" has found here a new version: "A human
being does not come into his own until he has become a
millionaire." An avalanche of bills has descended upon
the Congress at Washington that calls for the
expenditure of up to 100 million dollars for the
construction of an important naval force, the
augmentation of the standing army, the creation of
coastal fortifications and similar projects. How easily
even the workers march into the chauvinistic trap was
mentioned above in connection with Chicago.

Some time ago it was reported how Professor R. T.
Ely, now at the University of Wisconsin, after having
been investigated because of his economic teachings,
barely escaped being disciplined. His case by no means
stands alone. The American millionaires buy themselves

indulgences from all of their sins by gifts to
institutes and institutions as well as by donations to
schools and universities during their lifetime or in the
form of legacies after their deaths. These indulgences
contain the right to be protected from attacks in the
halls of ivy by the guardians of scholarship. The
rather numerous "Socialists of the Pulpit" at American
universities are embarrassed by this and if they are not
embarrassed, they are endangered. Professor Bemis of
the University of Chicago let his tongue have somewhat
free play in attacks (mostly of a petit-bourgeois sort)
upon the owners of communication, gas and other
corporations, particularly upon those who are located
nearby like the gas, streetcar, oil and other
millionaires of Chicago. The latter were displeased by
these attacks, particularly since they did not have an
equal defender on the spot, but the attacks seem to have
been even more disagreeable to Professor Bemis'
colleagues, particularly the president of the University
of Chicago (a president is similar to the rector
magnificus of the German universities) who complained to
Bemis in a letter that he could no longer show his face
in society or the country clubs, and who asked Bemis to
please move somewhere else. Bemis went--and
Rockefeller, the multimillionaire of the oil trusts
(Standard Oil Company) immediately gave the purified
university a million dollars with the promise that,
under certain conditions (which have since been
fulfilled), he would raise his donation to three million
dollars by New Years Day, 1896. For three million
dollars, or even one million dollars, it is worth it to
get rid of a professor. And the American bourgeoisie
does not even need a Herr von Köller to carry out such
purges!

14
The Presidential Election

1. The Republicans

The year 1896 is a leap year and in the United
States it is a presidential election year. The leap
year contains one more day than an ordinary year. The
presidential election year contains one or more
irritations, stupidities and wicked happenings. The
political life and the public devote themselves during
such years to the presidential election, concentrate on
turning out the vote, search for ways to rouse the
interest of the masses, and form and invent phrases to
bait the people. Everybody is out to win the favor of
the people!

First there are the conventions or assemblies of
delegates of the different political parties, the
contests of the nomination and the drawing up of the
program, or "platform" as it is called in America. Then
come the preparations for the election campaign: the
acquisition of money, the production of campaign
literature, the selection of the campaign orators and
their distribution around the various parts of the
country--all of this taking place for the most part in
July and August. Then follows the actual electoral
campaign, the great mass meetings, parades, debates,
etc. in September and October until the eve of the
elections. The election itself takes place on the first
Tuesday after the first Monday of the month of November,
between November 2nd and November 8th. This year it
will be on November 3rd.

Let us look first of all at the parties.

There are now three bourgeois parties in the United
States: the Republican, Democratic and so-called
People's or Populist Party.

The Republican Party is the party of the
bourgeoisie par excellence. Under its regime, American
industry became a rival of the Old World's industry.
The Republican Party worked for the protective tariff
system all the way to the McKinley Tariff, and it feeds
also upon the somewhat threadbare glory of having
abolished slavery. Under the rule of the Republican
Party, the American bourgeoisie has come to full bloom,
i.e., unrivaled public corruption. Under its aegis,
world-famous trusts were created and numerous
multimillionaires were born in the New World. Yes, one
can accurately claim that the Republican Party has made
incomparable achievements as far as the breeding of
millionaires is concerned. Therefore, the war chest of
the Republican Party is usually well-filled and not
easily exhausted, and thus it was not too difficult to
secure the necessary votes for gold currency during this
year's convention.
The Democratic Party, in general, constitutes the
party of the little man in the North and the party of
the white people in the South. A majority of the wage
workers of the North votes mostly for the Democratic
Party because (or whereas) their exploiters belong to
the Republican Party. In the South, the members of the
ruling white race, the old slave owners and their
retinue belong to the Democratic Party while the blacks
adhere to the Republican Party. It looks lately as if
the poor white population in the South might go over to
the Populist or Republican camps. The Democratic Party
has a free trade background, and it is for this reason
that the trading world favors it. High finance people
and the industrialists belong, with few exceptions, to
the Republican Party. The Southern states have until
now constituted the bulwark of the Democratic Party,
whereas the Western states and New England have formed
the stronghold of the Republican Party. Some middle
states in the East, such as New York and New Jersey and
several Midwestern states such as Indiana, Illinois and
Michigan have been the most contested areas in whose
hands the final decision commonly rested.
During the last few years, the Democratic Party has
been very much weakened by its inconsistent attitude in
Congress, and the people (that great ruffian) held it
responsible for the financial collapse of 1893 and the
subsequent commercial and industrial depression, so that
only a third of the members of the present House of
Representatives belong to the Democratic Party. In the
Senate, the Democrats are only able to accomplish
something with the support of the Populists and certain
silver Republicans. The Republican Party, on the other
hand, achieved a brilliant, land-slide victory in 1894
which assured it control over the House of
Representatives. In the Senate, the final decision
rests in the hands of the Populists since neither

Republicans nor Democrats have a majority there.   Into
this situation of the old parties, the currency
controversy has entered with a disintegrating effect
because it has infected both bourgeois parties to the
point of impending decomposition as may be gathered from
the course of the conventions.

Beyond the existing bourgeois parties, the
individual parts of the country have the following
attitude towards the currency question: for gold
currency are the New England states and the eastern
central states of New York, New Jersey, Pennsylvania,
Delaware and Maryland.   For silver currency are the
states of the Far West, especially the so-called silver
states of Colorado, Nevada, Idaho, Wyoming, Montana and
Utah, as well as the majority of the southern states and
Kansas and Nebraska.   Of the Midwestern states, Ohio,
Wisconsin and Minnesota lean towards gold, whereas
Indiana, Iowa, Michigan and Illinois are in doubt and
heavily contested.   These conditions present a similar
picture for both of the old parties.   Within the
Republican Convention, the Midwestern states of Ohio,
Illinois, etc., leaned from the very beginning towards
the wealthy East and gold currency, and the big
financial interests found it easy to buy up the Blacks
who make up the southern Republican vote. At this point
all of the others (except those from the silver states)
fell into line.   As far as the Democratic Convention is
concerned, there existed at first almost the same
relationship vis-a-vis the currency question as at the
Republican Convention, but New England and the eastern
central states remained isolated because the big
financial interests deserted them, in part, because they
had already won enough ground within the Republican
Party and, in part also, because the southern delegation
at the Democratic Convention (the ruling whites of the
old slave states) could not be had for a minor sum as
was the case with the recently enfranchised Blacks at
the Republican Convention.

To the two leading bourgeois parties (the
Democratic and Republican Parties) must be added a third
bourgeois party--the so-called People's or Populist
Party which arose during the past decade out of the
Farmers Alliance, a farmers' organization which had
developed in the Eighties.   In 1894 it had gained
approximately two million votes and in some states, such
as Kansas, Nebraska, Colorado, etc., it had achieved a
total or partial control and it had sent various members
to the Senate of the United States.   At first they
demanded only a safeguarding of agricultural interests
by the creation of federal storage facilities for
agricultural products and the limitation of railroad
privileges.   Wherever they were strong enough they made
life unpleasant for the mortgages by limiting their
privileges.   But in the end, they embraced, just like

the agrarian people of all countries, the panacea of
debased coinage and demanded silver currency so that
they could pay off their gold debts with silver.
    The origins of this new party go back all the way
to the Sixties, to the Civil War and the time
immediately thereafter. They may be found in the hatred
of the petit-bourgeoisie against the parvenu middle
class, the hatred of the then artisans, farmers and
grocers who were paid off with cheap paper money and
heavily taxed, against the capitalists who received gold
for their state securities and even were exempt from
taxation as far as these state securities were
concerned. The capitalists could also avoid service in
the war by paying money or buying a substitute. Out of
these dissatisfied elements arose at the end of the
Sixties the so-called Greenback Party (which wrecked the
National Labor Union) and its remaining members have
joined the present Populist Party. The growth of that
party in the western and southern states forced the old
parties to recognize it and, during the past few years,
to frequently enter into coalitions with it. In the
South it is the Republicans; in the West, the Democrats
who make common cause with the Populists. In the
Midwest, the Populist Party has gained little ground;
and in New England and in the central eastern states,
almost none. There the industrial workers are too
numerous and the proletariat has an instinctive aversion
to the debasing of coinage. The bulk of the Populist
Party is formed by the small farmers of the West who are
scattered from Kansas to Dakota and find themselves in
dire straits. They are joined by a large percentage of
southerners, and in different parts of the country petty
bourgeois citizens are making common cause with small
farmers.
    The first convention, that of the Republican Party,
was held between June 16th and June 20th at St. Louis, a
city which hardly three weeks before had experienced a
horrendous storm that had killed
hundreds of people and wrought damage in the millions.
The politicians could not care less but went ahead
putting their platform together. The platform first of
all lists a long register of sins supposedly committed
by the Democratic Party and then goes on to praise the
deeds of the Republican Party during the long years of
its rule. It (the Republican Party) "repeats and
emphasizes its adherence to the policy of protective
tariffs . . . in its responsible employment, this policy
is just, cheap and bi-partisan, opposing foreign
controls and native monopolies simultaneously"; the
renewal and expansion of the reciprocity treaties is
called for: "protective tariffs and reciprocity are the
twin measures of the Republican Party policy; protective
tariffs inject life into domestic industry and trade,
and secure the domestic market for ourselves--

reciprocity increases trade with foreign countries and
finds a market for our surplus." The current government
is accused of breaking its word in connection with the
sugar producers of the land (Louisiana); full protection
is promised to the producers of wool (the sheep raisers)
and for woolen goods, and the demand is made for the
rebuilding of the American merchant marine by erecting
differential tariffs and duties. "The Republican Party
backs without reservations the concept of 'sound money'.
. . . We will oppose uninterruptedly free silver coinage
unless it is accepted by international agreement with
the leading trading nations of the world. We pledge
ourselves to work for such an agreement. The existing
gold currency must be kept intact until such an
agreement is reached. All of our silver and paper money
must be maintained at an equal value with gold. . . . "
The veterans ought to be treated well and generously.
Our foreign policy ought to be always firm, forceful and
dignified, and all of our interests in the western
hemisphere must be carefully observed and protected.
"The Hawaiian (Sandwich) Islands should be controlled by
the United States and no foreign power will be permitted
to intervene there. The Nicaragua Canal ought to be
built, owned and run by the United States. The purchase
of the Danish Islands will secure a naval base in the
West Indies which is both very good and necessary."
There is a protest against the outrage in Armenia, and
American citizens and American property are assured of
full protection everywhere. The Monroe Doctrine is re-
affirmed. "We have not interfered in the affairs of the
current possessions of the European powers in this
hemisphere, and we will not interfere, but these
possessions must not be expanded under any pretext
whatsoever. We look forward to the eventual withdrawal
of the European powers from this hemisphere and the
eventual unification of all English-speaking parts of
this continent with the free consent of the
inhabitants." Sympathy with Cuba is expressed: "The
government of the United States ought to make every use
of its influence and its good services in order to
establish peace and create independence for the island."
Furthermore, the platform calls for the creation of a
strong navy, the strict enforcement of immigration laws
and the exclusion of all immigrants who can neither read
nor write, a protest is raised against the practice of
lynching, the creation of a federal mediation board is
called for to resolve conflicts between employers and
employees in interstate trading. A satisfactory
homestead law is demanded. "We sympathize with all wise
and legitimate efforts to decrease the evil of
incontinence and to further morality. The Republican
Party is aware of the rights and interests of women.
The protection of American industry includes equal
privileges and equal pay for equal work and the

protection of the home. We welcome the admittance of
women to greater spheres of useful activity, and we
applaud their cooperation in liberating this country
from misadministration and misgovernment."²   The
platform concludes "with the full confidence that the
election of the Republican Party will bring victory and
prosperity to the people of the United States."
    Senator Teller of Colorado tried to replace the
paragraph that deals with the money and currency matters
with a minority motion in favor of silver currency and
coinage, a motion which was rejected by a vote 818 to
105. After that, the entire platform was adopted
unanimously, whereupon the delegations of Colorado,
Idaho and Utah, and various delegates from Dakota,
Montana and Nevada, declared their withdrawal from the
Convention and left. In a rather long proclamation,
they tried to justify their conduct and win new
adherents to the silver currency. The well-known
protective tariff attorney, William McKinley of Ohio,
was thereupon nominated as candidate for the office of
the presidency by a great majority, and Garret A. Hobart
of New Jersey was nominated for the office of Vice-
President of the United States. During the spring, the
Manufacturers Association of the United States did a
great deal of work on behalf of McKinley and saw to it
that the overwhelming majority of the delegates received
binding instructions to vote for him. Because
McKinley's position on the currency question as well as
his activity in Congress on behalf of it had been most
ambiguous, the banking and trading world made a last-
ditch effort to create a counter-weight against the
person of McKinley, whom they disliked: the pushing
through of the paragraph dealing with the money and
currency question. With a certain wry humor it is
reported that it took from 50 to 500 dollars each to buy
up the Black delegates from the South so that they would
vote for "gold." "Respectable" Americans find the
candidature of McKinley unpleasant because during his
tenure as Governor of the State of Ohio, he personally
became involved in serious bankruptcy from which he was
only saved by friends and party members. The Republican
candidate for the office of Vice-President, G. A.
Hobart, is an influential politician and high-salaried
attorney from the railroads from the state of New
Jersey.

2.   The Democrats

    The Democratic Party held its convention from July
7th until July 11th in Chicago. The most influential
and respected man at the convention was Governor Altgeld
of Illinois. To him must be ascribed the content of the
platform. It is for many people an enigma how this

highly-respected, intelligent man could accept the
paternity of free silver coinage, and one can hardly
assume that it was merely his hatred and justified
contempt for the money bag idolizer and fat petty
bourgeois Cleveland that made him do that. His
extraordinary influence at the Democratic Convention was
a bitter pill to swallow for almost the entire big press
of the country which had heaped abuse upon him and
described him as a rebel, anarchist and revolutionary
ever since his amnesty and defense of the condemned
Chicago Anarchists (1898) and his attack upon President
Cleveland's intervention in the Chicago Railroad Strike
(1894). Next to him, all of the old politicians like
Hill and Whitney of New York, Cottison of Pennsylvania,
Gorman of Maryland, and others, were totally ignored.
Altgeld, even though a politician himself, appeared at
the Democratic Convention as the people's representative
in the genuine sense of the word. As no other person,
he deserves this recognition, which comes seldom to a
politician, because of his excellent administration of
the State of Illinois and also for his warm sympathies
for the interests of the workers. The last mentioned
consideration gained him (at the Democratic Convention
of Illinois which took place 14 days before on June
23rd) an unrivaled ovation and a brilliant, irrefutable
renomination which raised him far above the other great
figures of the Democratic Party in the entire country.
In his speech to the state convention at Peoria,
Illinois--in a sort of State of the Union Report--he
said among other things:
      "Four years ago our people were sitting under a
smiling sky. The country was tired of a government
policy (Republican) which made the few mighty and the
many poor. In Illinois, the population resented the
intervention of the state in the personal affairs of
individual citizens. On the federal level, we promised
a Democratic government and on the state level, we
promised an honest administration. The people believed
in us and gave us their confidence, and we conquered the
land with such a majority that a loyal adherence to
democratic principles could have secured for us a rule
of a quarter of a century. But even before the
inaugural ceremonies in Washington had ended, the head
of the new administration (Cleveland) turned towards
alien gods and fought for alien principles. He called
upon the advice of prophets who did not know democracy
or the principles of our forefathers. The people were
asked to bow before altars that they had formerly been
taught to beware of. The interests of money took
precedence over the interests of humanity. Organized
greed was fed with a golden spoon while the screams for
help on the part of the farmers were ignored, and the
sweat of the worker did not obtain bread for him . . . "

Of the state administration he said:
"Four years ago democracy made certain promises to
the people of this state. The people believed in them
and entrusted me with the government, and I am happy to
be able to tell you that as far as this state is
concerned, these promises have been loyally kept. The
able men and women who are connected with the various
departments of the state government have made every
effort to fulfill the high expectations that were
expressed towards them. All departments at the capitol
at Springfield, Illinois are in excellent condition. I
do not have the time to go into details, but the
institutions of our state, if viewed from a scientific,
business, progressive and humane standpoint, are
unsurpassed in the entire world, and every citizen of
this state, no matter to what party he belongs, can be
proud of it. . . . "
    He pointed especially to the reforms in the
administration of prisons and rejected the idea of being
renominated because his health was undermined. Also,
running the state had meant that he had to neglect his
private matters which had resulted in great financial
losses. He continued:
    "I have given the state four of the best years of
my life, and I have done the best that I could. I no
longer wish to run for any office. . . .I do not have
the ambition to be a party leader and to be prominent in
politics. . . . I am ready to do whatever I can to serve
my country . . .and I must therefore ask you to allow me
to retire. . . . " Unending applause followed Altgeld's
speech.
    What followed thereafter was reported to the
Illinois-Staatszeitung by an enemy of Altgeld in the
Democratic Party:
    "Altgeld was renominated for the office of governor
with the eruption of a truly unique wave of enthusiasm.
All delegates jumped up from their chairs, waved their
hats and broke out in seemingly unending cheers and
acclamations . . . seldom have I heard anything more
solemn and emphatic than the Governor's declaration that
he was against being renominated. If one disregarded his
erroneous comments on silver, one had to admit that he
rendered a most masterful description of the political
situation. When he came to the part where he said, 'I
am not in a condition to undertake another electoral
campaign because my health[3] is going downhill all the
time,' he was interrupted by loud shouts from all parts
of the building: You must, You must! And when he
concluded with the words, 'I would like to be relieved
from having to accept this nomination,' a tremendous
outcry arose from the audience which shouted: No! No!
No! Once the storm had subsided, the crowd broke into
cheers. The Governor observed the phenomenon with
visible emotion--it was obvious that he was deeply
moved. Anybody's chest would have been swelled with

pride had he been a part of such an honor that was the
product of the most sincere conviction. This honor was
the most convincing testimony of the Governor's ability
to be a leader of the people, and it illustrates the
esteem in which his followers and friends hold him . . .
    The Governor will accept the nomination."
    But back to the Democratic Convention!
    The program of the Democratic Convention begins by
coming out emphatically for freedom of speech, the press
and conscience; for the preservation of personal and
state's rights; and for the equality of all citizens
before the law. It mentions that the Constitution
refers to both gold and silver as the coinage metals for
the United States. It asserts that the law of 1873
which eliminated silver has raised the value of gold,
lowered the prices of all goods, increased taxes on
public and private debts, enriched the domestic and
foreign money lending class, paralyzed industry and
impoverished the people. The platform claims that to
adopt gold currency would be to follow British policy
which is out to make other nations financially dependent
on London. Such a policy is described as not only un-
American but anti-American and strangling the spirit of
independence and love of liberty won during the War of
Independence. "We demand the free and unrestricted
coinage of both metals, gold and silver, in the present
legal relationship of 16 to 1, without having to wait
for the assistance and approval of any other nation. We
demand that the standard silver dollar become a fully
legal means of payment, equal to gold, with which all
public and private debts may be paid. We favor the
issuance of such laws that will prevent in the future
the devaluation of any legal means of payment by private
contracts."[4] It should be up to the government to
decide whether debt certificates of the United States
should be paid in gold or silver. During peace time,
the government should not issue debt certificates.
Congress alone may coin and issue money and coins, and
the private banks should no longer have the right to
issue bills. The threatened re-introduction of the
McKinley Tariffs, which were twice condemned by the
people, disturbs business because it only breeds trusts
and monopolies, enriches the few at the cost of the many,
restricts trade and robs the producers of the great
American staple articles of access to their natural
markets. The program attacks the Supreme Court for its
annulment of the income tax and threatens to reverse the
judgement and transform the court so that just taxes may
be levied and wealth be properly taxed. American workers
are to be protected from competition by the prohibition of
the introduction of foreign pauperized workers. The
amassing of wealth in the hands of the few, the
consolidation of the big mighty railroads, and the
formation of trusts and monopolies are said to

require stricter supervision and control of the business
arteries by the federal government; the spendthrift
allocations of the past Republican congresses are said
to have resulted in unnaturally high taxes. "We condemn
the arbitrary intervention of the federal authorities in
local matters as a violation of the Constitution of the
United States and as a crime against free institutions,
and we declare our specific condemnation of government
by injunction as a new and highly dangerous form of
suppression by which federal judges, in violation of
federal laws and civil rights, become in one person
legislator, judge and executer." "We favor the
resolution of labor strife in inter-state business
through mediation and we recommend the issuance of laws
for this purpose." The Pacific railroads ought not to
be favored. Sympathy is expressed for Cuba "in its
heroic fight for freedom and independence." "We are
against life-long employment in public service and favor
hiring according to merit, restricted tenure and equal
opportunity for all citizens of recognized diligence."
The program demands the maintenance and improvement of
the navigability of the Mississippi and all large
waterways of the country by the federal government. The
platform concludes "with full confidence in the justice
of our cause and the necessity of its success at the
voting booth."

The notorious politician, Senator Hill of New York,
made two minority motions in favor of gold currency and
approbation of the Cleveland administration. Both
motions were rejected and the platform was accepted by a
vote of 628 to 301. William J. Bryan of Nebraska and A.
J. Sewall of Maine were nominated as candidates for the
office of President and Vice-President of the United
States. The delegations of New York, New Jersey,
Massachusetts, Connecticut and New Hampshire, either
totally or in part, refrained from voting.

William J. Bryan is a young attorney and politician
who is only 36 years old. He was twice a congressman,
has strong Populist tendencies, and is a talented
speaker. He owed his nomination to a brilliant speech
which he gave in support of the platform and against the
views of Hill, a speech which was received with
extraordinary enthusiasm by the Convention. Especially
effective were his words when he turned towards the
delegates from the East and said the following: "When
you stand before us and say that we have disturbed your
business interests, we reply that your actions have
destroyed ours. We are telling you that you have
defined the word 'businessman' much too narrowly. The
man who works for his wage is just as much a businessman
as the man who employs him." He achieved the greatest
effect, however, with the concluding words of his
speech: "You shall not crucify mankind upon a cross of
gold." The New York Herald remarked: "One phrase may

make a president." A special correspondent of the <u>New York Evening Post</u> who happens to be a vehement opponent of Bryan describes the latter as follows:

"Bryan has an untarnished record as far as his personal honesty is concerned. He won his first remarkable success by a speech dealing with the tariff question in the 52nd Congress[6] and he took a prominent part in the silver fight of the 53rd Congress. The discovery of his great ability persuaded the newspapers to turn him into a prominent person and ever since then, the House of Representatives has been more than willing to listen to his well-rounded phrases at any time and on any subject. Only a few orators have been honored this way in Congress. The result was that he gave up quite a substantial law practice in order to dedicate himself to journalism and politics, fields which seemed to offer a greater field of operation for his special talent. He is a homebody and his wife as well as his interesting group of children became well known during their sojourn in Washington. He is universally liked because his pleasant manners, even temper and respectful conduct never fail. In short, as a private person, he is an exemplary human being. His only fault lies in the public sector where his visionary ideas in politics make him out to be a Populist even though he is nominally a member of the Democratic Party. No vision is too fantastic and no project too difficult if he is convinced that it might aid the poor, the unfortunate and the incapable--even if it should result in exhausting the federal treasury."

The same correspondent states that the nomination of Bryan is generally regarded as a hopeful one.

A. J. Sewall is a wealthy shipbuilder and bank director at Bath, Maine.

3.   The People's Party

The Convention of the so-called People's or Populist Party was held at St. Louis from July 22nd until July 25th. It created special interest because of its relationship to the Democratic Convention. The universal question was: Will it come out for Bryan? The program of the Populists accuses the present administration as well as the previous ones of having created the current national crisis. It is necessary "to give back to the country the constitutional rights and controls that belong to a people's government but which have been ignominiously handed over by our public servants to the monopolistic corporations." "The influence of European money changers upon the legislation is more powerful than the voice of the American people, plutocracy reigns upon the ruins of democracy; in order to be masters of our own affairs and

in order to be independent of European control, only the
federal government, without interference by the banks,
may issue good, national and secure money as the legal
tender for all public and private debts". . . It
advocates "the unrestricted free coinage of silver and
gold in the present legal relationship of 16 to 1
without having to wait for the approval of foreign
nations; the quick augmentation of the currency to a
point where it will be sufficient for the needs of
business and the population and restore a just level of
work and production prices. The issuance of government
bonds by the present government is called both
unnecessary and illegal. The devaluation of the legal
money of the United States by private contracts is to be
legally prevented; the government is to pay for its
obligations in whatever money it wants to. "We demand a
graduated income tax so that the accumulated wealth will
bear its part of taxation, and we regard the most recent
decision of the Supreme Court on the income tax as a
misinterpretation of the Constitution and as an
intervention in the rightful powers of Congress in
matters of taxation." The Government ought to own the
railroads and run them in the interests of the people on
a non-partisan basis . . . The seizure of the railroads
is to be a gradual process in harmony with a sane public
policy. As soon as the mortgages are due to the federal
government, the Pacific railroads ought to be taken over
or acquired in public auction at reasonable prices, to
be administered and run for the benefit of the entire
people and not just a few. No renewal of the mortgages
of the Pacific railroads is to be permitted. The
telegraph system should belong to the government and be
administered in the interest of the entire people. Land
speculation, be it by railroads or other corporations,
by private individuals or foreigners, is to be
prohibited, and every settler is to be guaranteed a free
homestead (perhaps also in the Indian reservations which
are to be set up). Initiative and referendum, as well
as the direct election of the President, Vice-President
and the senators of the United States are demanded.
Warm sympathy and the wish to recognize their
independence is expressed towards the Cubans. In times
of crisis the unemployed are to be given jobs at public
works projects. Legislation ought to come out to
prevent judicial arbitrariness in the form of
injunctions and of arrests because of disrespect for the
law. The right to vote is to be protected. The
salaries of officials are to be determined by the price
of work and its products, etc., etc. At the end, the
importance and significance of the financial question is
once again emphasized, and all organizations and
citizens are asked for their cooperation and aid in view
of this vital question.

The convention was not at all unanimous when it came to the nomination of the candidates, and almost half of the delegates tended to proceed independently[7] whereas a bare majority demanded agreement between the Democratic and Populist platforms when it came to the main problem (the currency question) and, therefore, from the very first demanded the endorsement of the Democratic candidate. After long battles over this question, a compromise was made by which the presidential candidate of the Democratic Party, Bryan, was accepted for the Populist Party, too. The party, however, nominated its own candidate for the office of the vice-presidency: Watson of Georgia.

It should be pointed out that the old allies, the Knights of Labor, took an active part in the Populist Convention. Their Secretary and Treasurer of long standing, J. W. Hayes, served as secretary to the convention. From Wisconsin came the editor of the Populist-Socialist organ "Vorwärts" of Milwaukee and from Chicago came the praiseworthy and famous Henry D. Lloyd, but their efforts to make the platform more palatable and acceptable to the workers, was doomed from the start because E. V. Debs, the leader of the 1894 Chicago Strike, on whose influence they had counted and whose nomination had even been contemplated, did not appear.

Simultaneously with the Populist Convention (and in order to influence it) a convention of pure silver interests was convoked at St. Louis whose members were merely the wealthy owners of the silver mines of Nevada, Idaho, Montana, Colorado, etc. They limited their activities to working for Bryan's endorsement.

4.   The Prospects of the Candidates

The conventions are over. The parties and the candidates are preparing themselves. Let us take a closer look at the candidates and their followers, and let us also find out more about the West.

McKinley is not popular. Nowhere does his person inspire any confidence, but there are strong, very strong interest groups clustered around him and personal interests happen to be more powerful than personal sympathies. There are, first of all, the most active of them all: the protective tariff industrialists of New England, New Jersey, Pennsylvania, etc., and the numerous sheep raisers of Ohio and other states. As mentioned before, already by spring they had secured the majority of the state delegations for him because all of the efforts to raise the import duties were tied to his name. They were joined by the sugar producers of Louisiana with the demand for higher sugar subsidies in order to protect them against foreign sugar. On

July 30th, McKinley stated in a speech to such and
similar interests: . . . "The Republican Party . . .
believes in a tariff (i.e., custom law) which will lead
to an efficient and thrifty government which will serve
the highest and best interests of American labor,
American agriculture and American citizenship . . . we
believe that the custom question has been solved, solved
in the heart of the American people and solved in the
spirit of protection." On another occasion he declared
that it would be the first duty of the next Republican
congress to change the custom laws in the above-
mentioned sense, i.e., to render them protectionist.

The next big interest group supporting McKinley are
the members of the Grand Army of the Republic, veterans
of the Civil War, i.e., pensioners of the federal
government who obtain annually the sum of 150 million
dollars from the federal treasury, a sum of money
bequeathed to them by the Congress in which McKinley had
occupied a leading position. This interest group is very
powerful and numerous and has a membership of about one
million (McKinley himself gives an estimate of 970,000).
It can be estimated that there are about four million
voters who have an interest in these pensioners and
their pensions, which is certainly a respectable force
and is particularly powerful in New England and the
Midwestern states.

For McKinley are the big-producers, contractors,
owners of foundries, shipyards, etc., who rose under the
thirty year rule of the Republican Party and count on
the renewal of their contracts, on the augmentation of
the Navy, on an increase of the expenditures for river
and harbor construction, on the acquisition of new guns
and rifles, etc., i.e., they hope for a return of "the
beautiful days of Aranjuez."

On McKinley's side stand the jingos, the American
chauvinists and swaggerers, who advocate a forceful,
aggressive foreign policy for the United States as it
was carried out by Blaine under Harrison vis-a-vis
Chile, Hawaii, etc. Such a policy is directed
especially against England and Spain in favor of the
annexation of the Sandwich Islands, of Cuba and perhaps
other territory. The numerous military and naval
officers of the country who attended the academies of
West Point and Annapolis are under the influence of
McKinley.

McKinley is an American politician. The
politicians of the country as a professional class (and
in the United States there is such a class) are
generally for him, regardless of their party
affiliation.

High finance and the business world have been for
McKinley ever since they were able to insert the
currency paragraph into the Republican Platform. It has
already been mentioned that McKinley played an ambiguous

role in the currency question and the papers do not let
him forget it. Circumspect bourgeois papers call almost
daily for alertness during the elections to the House of
Representatives since one could not be sure of the
Senate or the President. When McKinley really talked
about gold at one time (a subject which he had long
avoided)--one such paper commented ironically: "Mister
McKinley should be congratulated because he has finally
gathered enough courage to pronounce the feared word
'gold'!
    The following excerpt from his speech of July 31st
reflects the hopeless vacuity of McKinley's speeches:
    . . . "I am glad to be able to receive as visitors my
old friends, neighbors and fellow citizens from. . . . I
have often visited your county in former years. I know
most of you personally. I know something of the stuff
your population is made of. I know something of the
spirit of your people. I know something of your loyalty
and faithfulness to the Union (of the United States)
during the war, and I know a lot of your loyalty and
faithfulness and patriotism when it comes to
administering our land in peacetime." And he continues
with: "I know, I am glad, I congratulate you" etc.,
etc. And such 'utter rot' is served up to the American
people and--is praised!
    William J. Bryan has a likeable personality which
can be said even more of his wife, whose congenial
character and good qualities are much talked about. He
is only one year older than the required age for an
American president, and this youth not only recommends
him to the youth of the country but the American people
in general, whose actions often betray youthfulness and
immaturity. There is no doubt about Bryan's oratorical
ability. His speech about the crown of thorns and the
cross of gold is supposed to have gained him innumerable
votes among the Americans who often succumb to the cult
of words. His youth is often reflected in the typical
American exaggerations that he often uses as, for
instance, in his speech of July 13th when he said: "This
is the greatest nation on earth. In my humble opinion
it has more of everything that makes a nation great. As
far as the important things are concerned, it is ahead
of all living and past nations. All that is offered to
the people here has led to the highest and newest
developments. We have the best form of government and
the most perfect form of government because we have a
government that can be as good as the people wish it to
be."
    The political rules of etiquette have until now
required that candidates for the highest office in the
land do not attack their political opponents personally;
that, as a matter of fact, they avoid mentioning their
names. Bryan, without compunction, ignores this rule
and wins applause when he says: "Mr. McKinley was the

most popular man among the Republicans and three months ago, everybody in the Republican Party prophesied his re-election. And what are the prospects today? (July 9th) The[8]man who used to boast that he looks like Napoleon, today shudders when he contemplates that he was nominated on the anniversary of the Battle of Waterloo. In his dreams he may hear from afar the noise of the waves that hit the lonely shore of St. Helena."

To those who mention that the big cities, the centers of trade and industry, are in favor of gold currency, he answers boldly and undauntedly: "You tell us that the big cities are for gold. Burn down your cities and let our farms stand: your cities will be resurrected and grow! But, destroy our farms, and the grass will grow in every city of the land."

5.   The Farmers of the West

The bulk of Bryan's followers is formed by the farmers, the small farmers of the West whose prosperity has been ruined by generally known causes and whose burden of debt has become unbearable. They are joined by the South of the country (except for Louisiana), in part because of the same reasons, but in part also because of old party loyalty and the old resentment against the North and East. Other followers of Bryan are the backwoodsmen of the silver states of Nevada, Idaho, Montana, Wyoming and perhaps also Oregon, Washington, Utah and California. For Bryan too, of course, are the silver interests of the country, the immensely rich owners of the silver mines--of whom several already occupy seats in the millionaires' club, the Senate of the United States, where they often cast a decisive vote. The silver people have given the nickname of "gold bugs" to the advocates of a gold currency, whereas a closer examination shows that as far as characteristics are concerned, there is very little difference between gold bugs and silver bugs.

The delegations from the central eastern and New England states which were so badly beaten at the Democratic Convention did not have the courage of the western silver delegations at the Republican Convention that rebelled openly and left the party. They feared the well-known reluctance of the Democratic voters to rebel against the party, and they knew that any such action would destroy any hope of further influence, preventing the acquisition of offices. Only individuals--to be sure, so-called prominent ones--have declared their decision to vote for McKinley, but in more recent days, the attempt is being made to persuade the so-called Gold Democrats to hold a separate nomination which, however, will hardly change the situation, i.e., the relationship between the contesting parties.

The fury of the old party horses of both Democratic
and Republican coloration over the innovators, the
destroyers of the old nimbus, is boundless and is
expressed in vituperations and accusations against the
new breed who are labeled Anarchists, Jacobins, rebels,
Socialists, revolutionaries, etc. Old Democratic party
organs such as the New Yorker Staatszeitung, The New
York Sun, The Illinois Staatszeitung and others,
renounced their ties to the party and asked their
readers to give their vote to McKinley.

The New York Sun, the organ of C. A. Dana, the old
Fourierist of Brook Farm and the consequent toady of the
notorious Tweed, stated on the day after the adoption of
the party platform at Chicago: "The agony is over. The
Democratic Party, legally convoked in its national
convention, pledges to re-introduce the coinage of
silver in its former relationship of 16 to 1 and to work
for the reimposition of an income tax. The democracy of
Jefferson, from which all ideas have been derived that
have given this land its political stability and
Republican stability and Republican enthusiasm, has
passed into the hands of those who are diametrically
opposed to Jefferson--the Socialists and Communists or,
as they are called here, the Populists. . . . " The
South is accused of apathy since the end of the Civil
War and the paper continues: "The seed of the Socialist
revolution was present in the South all along." The
article ends by saying: "The presidential candidate of
every Democrat who believes in honest money and who
still hopes that he can smash the enemies of all those
basic beliefs that have been instilled in him since
childhood, should be without any hesitation and wavering
for one man: William McKinley." There are prominent
papers--and not just the political or bourgeois foes of
the New York Sun--who dismiss the above-mentioned
pronunciation of the latter paper by pointing out that
for many a year all candidates of the New York Sun have
failed to win.

A delightful picture of the Populist delegates, as
well as a lovely example of the tone used by the organs
of respectability and decency towards their opponents,
is rendered by the following special dispatch of a New
York paper reporting from St. Louis on July 20th under
the following headline:

"Character of the Populist Convention
An Indescribable Pile of Wild-Eyed Agitators.
A Madness That Must Be Fought."

"When St. Louis offered its hospitality to the
Populist Convention, it wanted to obtain a show and it
certainly obtained one. Never before has such an
indescribable mob gathered within the confines of this
city. If only a few of the eastern Democrats, who

seriously contemplate letting their party be run by the
Populist elements of the West, could come here and take
a look at this assemblage, they would turn their backs
to the whole business and leave their party rather than
surrender. For students of physiognomy, these people
offer a great field of study. Long hair and unkempt
beards predominate. In most eyes exist dangerous glints
and almost every face lacks normality. Strange noses,
peculiar chins, uneven temples: everywhere lurk the
idiosyncratic and distorted. The only symmetric faces
in the mob belong to some of the leaders whose faces
express slyness rather than eccentricity. No agent of
dubious schemes would ever waste any words on them but
would immediately buy them. The craziest of the whole
bunch may be seen at the headquarters of the 'middle-of-
the-roaders' (the Populists who remain independent and
do not want to follow the Democratic Party). Only a few
of them reside in hotels. Nobody knows where they spend
the night. Not a clean shirt collar remains among them.
With their suits, they usually wear dark-colored calico
or flannel shirts. The broad-brimmed hat is another
staple article and the wilder the eyes, the more
extensive the brim of the hat. Unfortunately it is a
rabble that in spite of its clumsiness will not go away
when subjected to ridicule. For too long the East did
not pay any attention to it and will have to fight very
hard in order to overcome it. It is not the usual
rabble out of which mobs of plunderers and violators are
formed--rather it is a rabble that will use the lynch
law to defend what it considers its rights and its
system of social order. Just now this mob is caught up
in the idea that the East has robbed the West for years
and that the day of retaliation has come. It devotes
itself to the business of revenge with the eagerness of
the crusaders.
     The Convention is not representative in any sense
of the word. The bulk of its constituents consists of
the farmers who are a much better element. But the
farmers are at home, taking care of the harvest, and
they have sent these people to St. Louis because they
had the least to do in their communities and were the
best public speakers. These delegates can never be won
over to the cause of honest money. One has to meet them
on their own ground, in the presence of their own
people, and conquer them in open battle. The insanity
of their theory must not be exposed by high falutin'
oratory that goes beyond the mental range of the people
behind them, but by clear arguments. If promptly
undertaken, this task can be accomplished before
November. Negligence or the use of epithets instead of
arguments will bring certain defeat."
     The Neue Zeit has reported earlier about the
situation of the agricultural population in the West of
the United States, but eyewitness descriptions might

nevertheless be helpful. Specifically in regard to the
present political situation, a member of the bourgeois
class from the eastern state of Connecticut writes as
follows:

"I am personally very familiar with the situation
in the West because I lived for a year on the Pacific
coast and I spent many months in the towns of Iowa,
Nebraska, Kansas and Colorado. I am writing this letter
with a three-fold purpose: first of all, I want to
state that the people in the East generally have not the
slightest idea of the frightening changes that have
occurred during the past decade in the living conditions
of the above-mentioned states (and the adjacent ones).
I could tell story after story of people who fought a
long battle against crushing circumstances, or honorable
and highly conscientious people who finally, because of
the pressure, had to face bankruptcy and often death.
Furthermore, thousands have left their farms!   Ten
thousands of other farmers are defending themselves
desperately against the threatening public auctioneers.
The cause of this is no secret. Tenants of my own
farms, that have belonged to me from eight to ten years,
receive prices (for their products) that amount to
hardly half of what they obtained ten years ago. Mr.
Editor, I am asking you, therefore, to take all of these
circumstances into account if such suffering leads to a
tendency towards fanaticism.

I wish very much that the Eastern newspapers will
make an effort during this campaign to publish
quotations from the better (?) sort of Western
newspapers. One of the main reasons why the East has
not understood the depth and intensity of Western
dissatisfaction is the fact that we are too far away to
read its newspapers. Let us look, for example, at
Kansas. When I visited that state in 1885, I was
extremely surprised not only by its prosperity, but also
by the intelligence of its population in general. Even
its border towns were significantly more orderly than
similar towns in the East. There was not only
intelligence but also morality and a sense of community,
and obviously there was no prospect of introducing any
fanatical legislation which, with a certain amount of
success, has been tried since. But the rapid decline of
the price of beef in 1886 and 1887 and the subsequent
drop in price of wheat and oats (and practically
everything that the farmer plants) has created a slowly
rising mood which is illustrated by certain recent
Western comments. In the meantime, Kansas has become a
"bleeding Kansas"[10] in a new and different sense, and we
should keep this fact in mind.

Thirdly, I would like to appeal directly to the
editors of various Western newspapers because, at least
as far as one matter is concerned, they are themselves
guilty of contributing to the East's ignorance of the

affairs of the West. Recently I obtained a sample of a
Western newspaper of a town in whose suburbs I own 100
acres of land. I am thoroughly familiar with the
situation of the entire community whose business (trade
and industry), as in other parts of the West, are at a
complete standstill. Yet if one would judge the actual
situation according to this paper, one would think that
everything is hopeful and going great guns. In the
attempt to spread good cheer, to preserve the value of
property to lure new settlers, the editors have made the
error of misrepresenting the situation in the West. A
certain heroism marks this attempt and I give them
credit for it, but they must not be surprised that the
East does not understand the West if such misleading
news is reported."

In spite of its Philistine tone, one recognizes
everywhere in this letter the bourgeois sensibility and
bourgeois cowardice of the writer, whereas the following
epistle of a real Kansas farmer leaves nothing to be
desired as far as drastic expressions and bluntness are
concerned. It shows best the mood of the farmer in the
great West, their arguments and ways of speech. No
doubt, it is genuine! The man signs with his full name
and lists his home and mailing address. He writes to
the editors of the New York Evening Post as follows:

"Gentlemen! I am a constant and attentive reader
of the paper. I am a Democrat and a great personal
admirer of Grover Cleveland,[11] D. B. Hill and John G.
Carlisle. I know that John Sherman learns more in a
minute than I have learned in forty years and that
Russel and Whitney have forgotten more than I ever knew.
I am only an atom of mankind here in the middle of the
American desert and I have never seen during my entire
life a custom house or a mint. As far as financial
questions are concerned, I have never tried to persuade
anybody except myself, and even this seems to me to be a
hopeless task. I try to make myself believe that the
above-mentioned, excellent gentlemen know what they are
talking about in respect to the financial question--but
I cannot do so. I wish that I could, but it is unlikely
if not impossible. Not even the New York Evening Post
with its classical editors and editorials can make a
'gold bug' out of me.

I read many Eastern newspapers of great renown
which are edited with great skill and they make me mad.
I know of no newspaper in the East which, in my opinion,
has a real understanding for the expanse of this country
with its different needs and different currents of
thought on the part of the population. As far as these
questions are concerned, they (the newspapers) do not
live up to the requirements of the times. They call the
people of the West repudiators,[12] Anarchists and fools.
That is a serious error. The whole silver movement and
its demands do not aim at repudiation but the exact

opposite. The demand for more money is derived from the
wish to have something in order to pay off debts. A 53
cent dollar would only suffice to cover 53 cents worth
of debts. Many people in the East would be happy to get
as much. With a gold currency, they can never get as
much. The people of the West will pay 100 cents instead
of 53 cents and they believe that they will be able to
do so. They believe that a free coinage silver dollar is
worth as much. It is all very well to pay off debts in
gold, but it is devilishly difficult to persuade a
Western farmer that he can pay off his thousand dollar
mortgage with two hundred five-dollar gold pieces when
during the year he never gets to hold a single piece of
gold in his hands. It seems that the people in the East
truly believe that the people in the West consist of
Anarchists because of their demand for free silver. I
have lived for almost 20 years in the West and I have
never seen an Anarchist flag. I do not know what it
looks like. But I know that a person who would wave it
(the flag) would not live for more than 30 minutes. A
few years ago, we used to call the Populists Anarchists,
but it looks as if the people will storm towards them
like a herd of buffalo, carrying everything before them,
and that they will place them (the Populists) at the
head of the government. Indeed, neither ex-Governor
Glower (the former Governor of New York) nor a great
number of us know what the word Anarchist means, and
even if we know it, we do not use it properly. Most of
us should consult our Webster and also look up the word
"repudiator."
       The people in the West are no fools. I believe
that there are more people in a Kansas community (of
which there are many which are only sparsely populated)
that know more about economy and economic history than
similar communities anywhere else in the world. The
West studies economic questions very diligently. The
East does not know that and may be very disappointed at
the end of the campaign. No more than in Nevada[13] can
the proponents of gold currency win a single state west
of the Missouri River. Bryan will win Kansas with a
majority of 50,000 votes as surely as the sun rises in
the East. Kansas raises four pigs for every person, and
wheat, corn and other products grow in a similar ratio;
the people of Kansas want to have as much of a say over
the medium of exchange as New York, which raises only
one pig for every four people. The people of the West
are tired of being called fools, and one day they will
prove that they are not fools by exercising revenge by
exporting the immense amount of their products to the
South instead of New York, Boston, Philadelphia and
Baltimore.
       The newspapers of the East, in spite of all of
their erudition, use very lame arguments and the people

of the West are more amused than annoyed by their
efforts. New York journalism has yet to come out with
an editorial that convinces a Kansas man of his errors
if he has any erroneous ideas. If the Eastern
newspapers assert that the heads of the great railroads
and other enterprises understand the question and that
the Kansas farmer should accept their judgments, then
the farmers break out in laughter, take the statistical
tomes from the book shelves and enumerate the many great
railroads which during recent times ended up in the
hands of public receivership. The farmers truly believe
that the railroads are deeper into debt than any other
property of similar value and size. They state that the
Santa Fe Railroad, which is connected and equipped with
so many excellent financial experts, is in such bad
shape and so hopelessly indebted that its shares are
hardly worth the paper they are printed on. The farmers
used to regard the bankers as clever financial experts,
but while they (the farmers) held on to their farms,
they saw the bankers collapse all around them during the
past few years. They used to view Mr. Cleveland and Mr.
Carlisle as great financial experts but then they saw
how these gentlemen during the past two years plunged
the government into debt by nearly half of all the gold
that circulates in the country. The poor devil of a
farmer who must pay for freight is certainly not to be
criticized too much if he is determined through study
and contemplation to become just as good a financial
expert as a railroad magnate, a journalist or a
politician.

He (the farmer) also grows suspicious when the big
newspapers of the metropolis tell him that Bryan of
Nebraska is too young and inexperienced to direct the
country. He remembers that he has read somewhere that
Christ was much younger when he drove the money changers
from the temple; he knows that Thomas Jefferson was much
younger when he wrote the Declaration of Independence.
He knows that Napoleon was much younger when he led
France to the height of her glory. He knows that
Alexander was a dozen years younger when he had reached
the height of his fame, and he knows that Queen Victoria
was only half the age of Bryan when she began her
government under which occurred the development of the
greatest empire under the sun.

There are many Jeffersons, Napoleons, Alexanders
and Victorias in the West, and the country will hear of
them before they grow much older. The fathers of the
constitution who were clever and wise men did not
believe that a man of 36 years was too young for the
office of the president; otherwise, they would have set
a higher age limit. Some of my neighbors have told me
(and I do not know whether they are right or wrong) that
all of the bad laws in the body of laws have been
introduced there by much older men than Mr. Bryan.

Personally, I believe that both sides are too
radical and prejudiced. I believe that somewhere
something is wrong (or rotten) and I would like to see
both East and West more reasonable. It would be good
for both sides to learn how to understand each other and
to do business as friends and citizens of the same
country. If the East could only imagine that the people
of the West are not all Anarchists, fools and
repudiators, and if the West could be persuaded that its
Eastern cousins are not all thieves, shylocks and
plutocrats, then both parts could be brought closer
together. The man of the West is not necessarily a man
of silver. His demand: enough money so that he can
take care of his agricultural business. If you give him
that, he will not give a hoot whether it consists of
gold, silver, or paper."

These three pieces of writing, the report by the
journalist, the appeal of the petit bourgeois and the
fresh battle cry of the farmer from Kansas, render an
excellent picture of the situation in the West, the most
aggressive part of the country, and with which the South
will probably advance in unison against the East. It is
in the East that high finance, the trade world and big
industry are concentrated, and the West will make every
effort to recapture the decisive centers: the states of
Ohio, Indiana, Illinois, Michigan and Wisconsin. The
small farmers are in a state of rebellion against the
conditions as they are being maintained by the
bourgeoisie. The farmers mean business because they are
in dire straits. In their shortsightedness they demand
that which lies nearest at hand: more money. It is
certain that even the obtainment of their main demand
will hardly improve this situation, and that they will
not recover by the introduction of free silver coinage.
After a brief recovery, the disadvantages of a silver
currency will make themselves felt towards the producers
of raw materials and in general against all those who
produce. The small farmers no longer have a future,
which is not to be regretted at all because the labor
movement of the United States will only grow healthy and
rise after the small farmers' movement is finished. In
case of a victory for the silver currency, the
bourgeoisie, the bearer and dispenser of the system of
exploitation, will have to overcome a few minor
inconveniences but it will increase its profits and
augment its property just as much as under a gold
currency.

This year's electoral battle, as it is being fought
by the farmers of the West, has many a congenial aspect
for the unbiased observer.

The farmer fights for his existence as a working
man as well as the owner of a piece of land, and if he
does not find the cause of his oppressed situation and
his misery in the predominant mode of production but in

the workings of the world market, the anti-collectivist skull of the farmer should no more be looked down upon than the anti-socialist skulls of the industrial workers of the country who are either, as Knights of Labor, allied with the Populists or, as members of the American Federation of Labor, supporters of the silver currency at a rate of 16 to 1.

The Farmers of the West also battle with the bureaucracy that is particularly entrenched in the judicial and tax systems. They fight against creeping nepotism and all of the old politicians, which is not to be understood, however, as a fight against all politicians because they and their leaders are, after all, politicians themselves. They only assault that which is old, traditional, ancient and respectable, and they confront it with their youth, freshness and freedom. The crude and the rough battle those of good manners and those steeped in culture.

The corpulent occupants of offices and chairs find themselves pressed against the wall by the youth of the great plains along the Mississippi and the Missouri who impatiently demand recognition as do the weather-beaten pioneers of the Rocky Mountains.

The poor indebted farmers of the West are rising up against their creditors in the big cities of the East. Therefore the slogan: "The Poor against the Rich" has emerged.

The Stock Exchange registers all of this and betrays signs of irritability.

What will be the result? Probably what was hinted at before and predicted by Engels several years ago: A thorough explosion that will cleanse the air and which will teach the Americans a lesson which will make them wise!

Chapter XIV: Endnotes

[1] The platform is so long that only the most important parts are rendered here verbatim.

[2] A reference to the events in Colorado and elsewhere, where women had voted against the Populists.

[3] Altgeld suffers greatly from physical ailments.

[4] This stipulation is directed against the clause in purchasing and renting contracts, mortgages, etc., that specifies that the payment must be made in gold.

[5] This refers to the intervention of federal judges in the Pullman Strike of 1894 and its suppression by injunctions.

[6] The period of tenure for every congress is 2 years. The 52nd, 53rd, and 54th congresses all were congresses whose periods of tenure lasted until the 104th, 106th and 108th year since the writing of the Constitution.

[7] They were and they are called "middle of the roaders" because they move neither to the right nor to the left but stay "in the middle of the road."

[8] McKinley allegedly has a great resemblance to Napoleon and is, therefore, often called Napoleon McKinley.

[9] Private letters of people from Kansas, Dakota and other states confirm this news.

[10] "Bleeding Kansas" was a party battle cry in the middle of the 1850s when there were frequent bloody clashes over the extension or prohibition of slavery in Kansas and Nebraska, a conflict in which John Brown played a prominent role.

[11] Grover Cleveland, the present President of the United States; D. B. Hill, Democratic politician and former Governor of New York; J. G. Carlisle, Secretary of the Treasury; John Sherman, Senator and also a former Secretary of the Treasury; Russel, a former Governor of Massachusetts, Whitney, millionaire and politician, all of them prominent politicians and Democrats except for Sherman who is Republican.

[12] In America, people are called repudiators if they do not recognize their obligation to pay off a debt (particularly a debt to the state).

[13]Nevada is a strict silver state, or better, a silver mining state. It has the least number of inhabitants of any state.

15
Strikes and the Progress of Socialist Party

Politics, i.e., bourgeois politics--the presidential elections--, cause the greatest commotion, and the claim is made that the welfare of the country depends on them just because they decide bourgeois questions. Often however, their insignificance is highlighted and their pretentious claims rejected by the commotion within the so-called lower strata and by developments within the circles of organized and unorganized labor. An outstanding example of this was the Presidential Election Year 1892 with the insurrections and strikes of Homestead, Couer D'Alene, Buffalo and Tennessee; the current year, too, offers enough examples to show that a considerable number of workers do not forget their more important interests while considering national politics.

At the beginning of May a general strike of Tramway employees occurred in Milwaukee, a strike which created a tremendous sensation in the entire country because of the unanimity of support rendered by the entire population which stood at the side of the strikers. When the Tramway Corporation refused to take into account the modest requests of the workers, refusing even to consider them, the workers called for a boycott of the entire network of the company and probably never before was a boycott carried out in such a strict and cheerful manner by the entire population of a large city. As a matter of fact, the exploitative Tramway Corporation would probably have been defeated and expropriated had it not been for bourgeois offices, officials, courts, governors and articles of law. After a duration of about six weeks, the strike ended in defeat; capital had proven mightier than labor because it was supported by all similar companies in the country. The newspaper Vorwärts, published in

Milwaukee, wrote about it in mid-June:
  "The Milwaukee tramway strike and boycott which has
just ended is one of the most phenomenal and epoch-
making events of the labor movement. For over a month,
the 160 large, beautiful, comfortable cars which are
equipped with all modern conveniences, ran from early in
the morning until long past midnight with no passengers
except policemen who rode along for protection, and this
was happening in a city which, due to its cottage system
(small homes with some space around them), covers a much
greater surface than an Eastern U.S. or European city
with the same number of inhabitants. For more than four
weeks, the workingmen battalions walked daily to and
from work even though the distances were often so great
that one could see large groups of male and female
workers sit and rest along the sidewalks.
  All of our respect goes for this expression of
solidarity on the part of Milwaukee's workers!
  It cannot be denied, of course, that there existed
other factors that contributed to this magnificent
boycott, namely the hatred of the petit-bourgeoisie
towards monopoly capitalism, the general bitterness over
the ruthless conduct of monopoly capitalism when it
abolished the sale of 25 tickets for one dollar, hurried
through special bills in the legislature in order to
evade taxes, etc.
  The boycott, however, was primarily the achievement
of the working class which had been trained for a number
of years by the most vivacious political agitation of
the Socialists (during the last elections 9,300 votes
were cast for a party platform which was described by
the Populist leader as "suicidal"). The Socialists had
at first argued against the strike, but once it had been
decided upon, they supported it with all of their might
and, during the first four weeks, constituted its very
soul. By the way, the strikers themselves must be
praised because they held together until the end with a
show of discipline that one rarely finds among ordinary
unskilled workers."
  On May 1st of the current year, the organized
workers of the Brown Hoisting Works in Cleveland, Ohio
made diverse demands, e.g., the introduction of the
nine-hour day, a half-day holiday on Saturdays, a small
raise and a mediation board in case of conflict--all of
this constituting the recognition of the union. The
negotiations were of a prolonged nature, but in the end
the labor participants--machinists, iron workers and
carpenters--were locked out and a hard fight ensued
because management intended to see the jobs of the
locked-out workers filled by scabs. The police were
powerless in the face of the pressure of the masses who
sympathized with the locked-out workers. The militia
was called out, too, but it found itself almost as
helpless as the police. Clashes were frequent, several

people were hurt, a man was killed, and finally the
company conceded to all demands; but it took back only a
few of the old workers. The principle was saved, but
the workers had to foot the bill.

In New York a new strike broke out in July among
the mostly Jewish male and female workers in the garment
industry. These strikes have become almost chronic but
recently the strikers have suffered from fragmentation
into diverse Anarchist, Socialist or purely unionist
factions. Small successes were achieved nevertheless,
and the proletarians for the most part enjoyed free days
during the hot summer time.

In July the window glass workers held their annual
convention. They have a superb organization to which
belong 5,000 to 6,000 workers of this trade which, until
now, formed a part of the Knights of Labor under the
name of "Assembly Nr. 300". They are inveterate
protectionists and thus support McKinley. At their
convention they declared that they would quit the
Knights of Labor because that organization cooperates
with the Populists, i.e., it has become identified with
it. McKinley personally addressed 300 glass workers
with a protectionist speech.

The legislatures of the country were careful not to
launch any attacks against the workers during this
presidential election year but, on the other hand,
nothing remarkable was done in favor of the working
class because the ruling class felt too secure. In New
York, however, due to the influence of philanthropic men
and women, two laws were issued that are worth
mentioning. The first law calls for the opening of an
unemployment office, an institution which has existed in
all larger towns in Ohio for three years and which has
been copied in other western states. The State of New
York is merely giving the matter a try. It has granted
$5,000 for a try-out and restricted its expenditure to
the City of New York. On July 20th the office was
opened with a supervisor and three assistants. The
following report about its opening has been written:
"About a hundred people were standing in line before the
office was opened (9 o'clock). There were only a few
women amongst them. Some of the people were very old,
but the average age was about forty. Most of them
seemed to be decent workers. Only a few wanted to admit
that they had been unemployed for more than three
months. On the average, they admitted to having been
unemployed from ten to fourteen days. Many applicants
were skilled workers--especially carpenters."

The second law, which was pushed through by women
and women's leagues, rightfully deals with worthy
measures for the protection of boys, girls and women in
mercantile establishments, especially the gigantic
modern bazaars. A big, strictly capitalist, newspaper
made the following comment concerning this law: "The

entire community has an interest in this subject.
Excessive work and excessive fatigue as well as a lack
of cleanliness touch upon health, and the health of its
(the community's) women and children is a matter of
great importance. An unhygienic environment for women
will affect the health of their children. Children that
have been raised and educated without regard to their
health, will later on become unhealthy parents. The
poison (virus) continues to spread with each new
generation." The writer of the citation is sorry that
he has to move so far away from the principle of
laissez-faire but he adds that "health is similar to
morality--it is of the highest imaginable common
interest, and the judicial system may declare agreements
illegal which are contrary to health (contracts contra
sanitatem) just as it may refuse to enforce contracts
directed against good morals (contracts contra bonos
mores)." The ordinary bourgeois, whether American or
European, pays attention to matters of public health
just as he concerns himself with matters of railway
safety. After all, he suffers as much as the workers
from unhygienic conditions, and he appreciates his life
and limbs at least as much as the proletarians. In the
United States there exist almost everywhere boards of
health who devote themselves to sanitary and hygienic
matters and exercise practically sovereign power. The
boards of health of New York City and other towns
received the following instructions:
     No child under 14 years of age can be employed by a
commercial establishment.
     No male under 16 years of age and no female under
21 may work for more than 10 hours a day or 60 hours a
week. They may not work before 7 a.m. and after 10
p.m., except during Christmas (i.e., almost the entire
month of December). Seating opportunities, bathrooms
and toilets are to be provided. Only under special
circumstances (sufficient light and air) may children
and women work in basements, and the lunch break must
last at least 45 minutes.
     That the miners of the West, particularly all those
that dig for ore, are an active and tough bunch was
formerly proven by the events in Idaho, Tennessee and
Colorado (Cripple Creek) which at times was marked by
tough action. During recent times, these people are
stirring once again very actively in one of the most
significant mining districts of Colorado at Leadville.
As far as the gentlemen owners of the mines (primarily
corporations) and their managers and superintendents are
concerned, the situation in said district, (as well as
in many others of the Far West) is especially unpleasant
in case of labor disputes because not only do the miners
control their district as inhabitants and voters by
electing all officials, but also they are strict union
people, i.e., members of their special union. The

following news from Leadville is most interesting because
it illuminates the present situation: "Leadville,
Colorado, September 16th.   The Miners' Union has made
public a declaration in which it offers to rent, work and
drain all mines of the lower town, to pay the owners 25%
royalty and 3 dollars a day for their work (the low pay
scale is what they are protesting against).   It (the
union) offers a collateral of 100,000 dollars if the
agreement is carried out. . . ."

The Socialist Trade and Labor Alliance (S.T.L.A.),
which was founded last December, held its first
constituent convention in New York. The official report
lists the presence of 68 delegates (of whom several held
mandates to the Congress of the Socialist Labor Party)
from the cities of New York, Philadelphia, Newark (New
Jersey), Boston, Buffalo, Brooklyn and Yonkers.   The
proceedings reverberated with attacks upon the existing
old labor unions and associations.   One speaker declared:
"The American Federation of Labor and the Knights of
Labor, or what is left of them, are only appendices of
the repressive machinery which is used by the capitalist
class against the working class."   Another speaker
referred to "the decline and worthlessness of the Knights
of Labor and the American Federation of Labor."   However,
the following passage from the Constitution, Article 2E,
must be juxtaposed to these comments: The purpose of the
Socialist Trade and Labor Assocation is to establish
"friendly relations with other bodies of organized labor
both at home and abroad and to cooperate with them
wherever possible."   A complete constitution was worked
out and adopted.   What must be said right away of this
document is the fact that it has copied as much as
possible of the terminology of the Knights of Labor and
that it excludes any member that belongs to any party
other than the Socialist Labor Party.   The convention
warned the workers of the United States not to take a
stand on such political questions as the so-called
reform, the currency, the duties and taxes.   A committee
was appointed in order to persuade the Congress of the
Socialist Labor Party to endorse the Socialist Trade and
Labor Association and a delegate was sent to the
International Trade Union Congress in London.

The Congress of the Socialist Labor Party met in New
York from July 4th until July 11th. There were about 100
delegates from California, Connecticut, Illinois,
Indiana, Iowa, Maryland, Massachusetts, Missouri,
Nebraska, New Hampshire, New Jersey, New York, Ohio,
Pennsylvania and Rhode Island.   New York alone sent 37,
New Jersey 20 and Massachusetts 13 delegates.   The very
comprehensive report of the national executive committee
gives an overview of the socialist successes in other
countries, touches upon the death of Friedrich Engels and
then confirms the success of agents that had been

sent out to establish new sections of the party. It
then reads: "As was to be expected, not all of the
sections survived after the organizer had departed, but
enough of them remained in order to render the
organizing work extraordinarily valuable. . . ." The
general situation is described as follows: "This year's
political situation is most promising for a considerable
progress of our movement. . . . The events which will
occur after the nomination of the presidential candidate
of the Socialist Labor Party may not happen in exactly
the way it has been predicted above but, enough of it
will come true. . . . If we examine the economic phase
of the labor movement, we find that the peculiar,
antiquated form of labor organization, the "pure and
simple union," has reached the end of its effectiveness.
. . . The pure and simple union is no longer an
organization that can still pretend to improve the
situation of its members by fighting the bosses
(employers) that want to worsen its situation. Instead
of fighting the capitalists, they limit themselves to[1]
fighting the poor devils that are no longer employed.
They have sunk to constituting a mere social welfare
society which relieves the capitalist class from
worrying about its victims and it seems that the only
benefactors of these social welfare organizations are
the labor fakirs who grow fat on the shoulders of those
that they fool . . . but there is a silver lining in
those dark clouds: The Socialist Trade and Labor
Alliance has been created. . . . " The hope is
expressed that the Socialist Trade and Labor Alliance
will be emphatically endorsed although there are
comrades "who favor a hesitant and non-binding position
on behalf of the party." State level organizations
exist in California, Illinois, Iowa, Massachusetts, New
Hampshire, New Jersey, New York, Ohio, Pennsylvania and
Rhode Island. There exist 200 sections in 25 states, of
which there are 40 in New York, 27 in New Jersey, 26 in
Massachusetts, etc. "It is difficult to estimate the
membership, but it can be asserted that it lies between
5,000 and 6,000people." A separate national committee
was formed in Canada. The Socialist vote has grown
satisfactorily in Paterson (New Jersey), in Holyoke
(Massachusetts) as well as in Brooklyn and New York.
"The party was less successful in the interior of the
state (New York). In some towns the number of votes
increased, in others it decreased even where sections
existed." The deficit which had been caused earlier by
the press organs of the party have ceased; "The People"
has developed excellently and possesses currently a
healthy financial basis. It constantly penetrates new
circles and has become a power in the land. . . . " The
founding of a daily Socialist newspaper is desired. "A
further official party organ was then born: the Jewish
Arbeiterzeitung in New York." A Scandinavian and a

Dutch organ are mentioned. An Italian and a Polish
newspaper, and diverse others, existed for a short time.
"Our Jewish comrades have founded a very successful
daily paper which sells for one cent. The Abendblatt
has a circulation of 15,000." Long controversies
emerged over Labor, a journal published in St. Louis,
and the convention was asked to take steps against it.
The suspension of the sections in Toledo and Cleveland
were justified, and a protest registered against the
decision of the executive council in the affairs of
another section (Syracuse). The convention was asked to
render its judgement on the activity of the national
executive committee "but to take into account when
judging that today in the entire labor movement of
America there is only one rallying point in the darkness
and only one existing harbor on the ocean of pessimism:
The Socialist Labor Party. As a result of this policy
and its clear declaration of the principle of
proletarian class struggle, the movement has kept its
equilibrium, and our offensive is holding the red banner
aloft, offering defiance to our foes and extending a
welcome to our friends; we are what we should be:
America's fighting Social Democracy.
     The most important issue of the negotiations was
the proposed endorsement of the new trade union league,
the Socialist Trade and Labor Alliance. It was fought
especially by the delegates of the City and State of New
York and the cities of St. Louis and Philadelphia, but
finally the proposal was accepted by a vote of 70 out of
77. A peculiar phenomenon occurred when several of the
most vehement opponents of the Socialist Trade and Labor
Alliance, as well as the most vehement speaker against
the endorsement, voted for it when it came to the actual
vote. Many delegates protested against the tactics used
by the New York adherents and founders of the Socialist
Trade and Labor Alliance, but they, too, voted for the
endorsement. The passage from the constitution which
reads: "We recommend all Socialists to join the unions
of their respective trade" was eliminated and replaced
by: "It was decided that every year three delegates
will be elected to attend the Convention of the
Socialist Trade and Labor Alliance." This change was
approved by 58 out of 69 votes. The paper, Labor, which
is published in St. Louis, was disavowed, the connection
of the party with the Jewish working class papers
Arbeiterzeitung and Abendblatt was dissolved,² New York
is once more the seat of the national executive, and
Cleveland has been designated as the seat of the board
of trustees. Charles H. Matchett of Brooklyn and
Matthew Maguire have been nominated to the offices of
President and Vice President of the United States.
     The Congress, which had experienced some hot
controversies over the Socialist Trade and Labor

Alliance as well as the change in the election of the
executive, concluded in the evening of July 11th with a
parade and a ratification ceremony in Union Square in
New York.

The proceedings of the Congress caused great
dissatisfaction in St. Louis, and within the New York
section, the strongest in the country, there was for a
long time unrest and perturbance over the Socialist
Trade and Labor Alliance.

The program of the Socialist Labor Party, which was
adopted by the national convention in New York on July
9th, reads as follows:

"The Socialist Labor Party of the United States,
represented by its national convention, declares once
again 'the right of all men to life, liberty and the
pursuit of happiness.'[3]

In unison with the founders of this Republic, we
are convinced that it is the purpose of the state to
make sure that each citizen may exercise that right.
But in view of the social conditions, we are also
convinced that such a right cannot be exercised under
the rule of a system which destroys life, liberty and
happiness.

In unison with the founders of this Republic, we
are equally convinced that the only genuine political
system consists of the people owning and controlling the
entire administrative machinery. In view of our economic
development, we are similarly convinced that in any
genuine economic system, the people also own the entire
machinery of production.

From the irreconcilable contrast that exists
between our economic despotism and our political
democracy originates naturally the development of a
privileged class; the corruption of the government by
this class; the transfer of the people's property, of
public justice and other public functions to this class;
and the humiliating dependence of the mightiest of
people on this class.

By the degeneration of democracy into a plutocracy,
the production of goods (which they alone create) is
robbed of the possibility of procuring for them their
own work and bread, yes, even satisfying their most
basic needs, and they are plunged into a condition that
offers them merely the choice between unemployment and
wage slavery.

Thus human and natural resources are wasted so that
the money bag may rule.

Ignorance and misery, and all of the sufferings
that follow in their wake, are promoted so that the
people may not shake off their chains.

Science and the inventive spirit, instead of
serving mankind, are misused for the enslavement of
women and children.

The Socialist Labor Party decisively protests, in
the name of liberty and justice, against such a system
and declares once more its fundamental principle: that
the private ownership of the natural sources and means
of production is the obvious cause of wage slavery and
the political dependence of the masses.

With gigantic steps the time is approaching when,
in the natural course of social development, the
existing social system will have prepared its own
downfall by causing on the one hand negative destruction
by ruin and crisis, and on the other hand negative
construction by the tendency towards trusts and
capitalistic combinations. We, therefore, call upon all
workers and all honorable citizens of the United States
to organize themselves under the banner of the Socialist
Labor Party into a class-conscious body which, conscious
of its rights, has decided to acquire these rights by
seizing public power; so that, in spite of the most
difficult circumstances of the present class struggle
and united by an unshakable spirit of solidarity, we may
put a summary end to this barbaric fight by the
abolition of classes. Thus we will give back to the
people in its totality the land and all the means of
production, transportation and distribution; and the
current planless production, the industrial strife and
social disorder will be replaced by a cooperative
community system. What will emerge will be a community
in which every worker will enjoy self-determination and
the full benefit of his abilities augmented by all of
the factors of modern civilization.

Resolutions

In an effort to improve immediately the conditions
of work, we make the following demands:

1. A reduction of working hours commensurate with
    the progress of production.

2. A take-over by the federal government of all
    railroads, canals, telegraphs, telephones and
    other means of communication that stretch
    across the land. The employees will run them
    collectively under the control of the federal
    government. They will elect their own
    supervisors and no employee may be dismissed
    for political reasons.

3. The take-over on the part of the community of
    all urban trains, ferries, water works, gas
    works, electrical installations as well as the
    monopolies and industries for which urban
    licenses are required. The employees run them
    collectively under the control of an urban

administration and elect their own
supervisors. No employee may be dismissed for
political reasons.

4.   No public lands may be sold. All land
      donations to corporations and individuals may
      be revoked if the conditions connected with
      these donations, have not been met.

5.   Only the United States has the right to issue
      money.

6.   The regulation of the forest and water systems
      according to scientific principles and the
      prohibition of the wastage of natural
      resources by federal legislation.

7.   The release of all inventions with a guarantee
      of national rewards for the inventors.

8.   A progressive income and inheritance tax with
      freedom from taxation for people with low
      incomes.

9.   Universal obligation to attend school until
      the completion of one's fourteenth year and
      free school attendance for those without means
      as well as public assistance (like meals,
      clothes, etc.) in all institutes of learning.

10.   The abolition of all pauper, tramp, conspiracy
      and limitation laws. Unlimited freedom to
      form coalitions.

11.   Public statistical inquiry into working
      conditions. Prohibition of child labor during
      the age of obligatory school attendance and
      the prohibition of all female work injurious
      to health and morality. The abolition of the
      contract system for the work of prisoners.

12.   The employment of the unemployed by the public
      authorities of the cities, counties, states
      and the federal government.

13.   The payment of wages in the currency of the
      United States and laws that ensure equal pay
      for equal work by men and women.

14.   Laws for the protection of the lives and
      health of workers and an effective liability
      law.

15.   The rights of the people to propose

legislation and the holding of plebiscites in
case of all more important bills.

16. Abrogation of the right to veto wherever it
    exists on the national, state and county
    level.

17. Abolition of the federal senate and all other
    upper chambers of law.

18. Communal self-administration.

19. Equal and direct right to vote by secret
    ballot regardless of any difference in race,
    nationality or sex. The introduction of the
    principle of proportional representation.
    Legal designation of all election days as
    holidays.

20. The possibility of recall for all members of
    the legislative bodies.

21. A uniform civil and criminal law within the
    United States. Free administration of
    justice. The abolition of the death penalty.

From Chicago arrived the following report during
mid-July:
"At the beginning of the year, there was a lot of
talk that the unions would resume their offensive to
gain further advantages, but at the beginning of spring
everything turned out to be very, very quiet. The only
strike of importance which we have had so far this year
was lost after a battle of ten weeks. I am speaking of
the strike of the tailor's cutters.
"Only a few years ago, the tailor's cutters were
regarded as part of the labor aristocracy, and now they
belong to the very common working class proletariat.
The 'bad times' have brought this about. One says 'bad
times' because the workers and the petit-bourgeoisie
still do not want to admit that they have sunk once
again a step lower during the last years. But let us
turn to the strike.
"Until January the minimum wage of the tailor's
cutters was 18 dollars; that of the trimmers (they
prepare the lining, etc.) was between 14 to 16 dollars a
week. The clothing manufacturers had been waiting for a
long time for a favorable opportunity to get rid of 'the
tyrannical supervision' of the union. The union
insisted upon a minimum wage and also insisted that a
piece worker can only cut a certain amount of cloth per
day. The tailor's cutters are seasonal workers and, on
the average, have steady work for only six months of the
year, so that their wages, if calculated on an annual

basis, are very modest. In January the union demanded a
minimum weekly wage of 20 dollars, a demand which was
generally rejected by the producers so that small
strikes broke out here and there. There are about two
dozen clothing manufacturers in Chicago. Acting in
agreement with the clothing manufacturers of other
cities, they made the following demands of their workers
at the end of February: 'The manufacturers employ and
dismiss their workers at their discretion, the wages to
be reduced to their former level.' What that means is
explained by the fact that the tailor's cutters
'formerly' received 12 to 13 dollars and the trimmers 8
dollars weekly. But that was not all. Not only were
the salaries to be considerably shortened but the rate
of work was to be mightily increased. In the future,
certain types of cloth were to be layered tenfold
instead of sixfold--we are dealing here with cloth that
is cut with a knife. Cloth that is cut with scissors
was formerly placed in double or triple layers--now it
is supposed to be placed in four-fold layers.
    "The acceptance of these demands would have been
tantamount to the complete dissolution of the union and
thus a strike occurred. The union contained 900 working
members and 400 tailor's cutters who were unemployed.
Nearly all of the workers belonged to the union. At
first, the workers were certainly confident of victory.
During the second half of March the majority of tailors
(there are about 25,000 here) also went on strike. Now
matters became much more tense. The usual guerrilla war
developed in which the police intervened. Well-meaning
people gave orations and the misery of the tailors was
treated sensationally by the press--all phenomena which
may be observed during any mass strike but are hardly
conducive to stopping the course of events. At the
beginning of May the defeat of the workers was complete.
    "Now the union has naturally shrunk considerably.
Once the workers had recognized that the battle was
lost, the ranks of the fighters were growing sparser.
The vanquished suffered insult in addition to injury.
Former union members sent the union after the defeat the
following note that they had, of course, not composed:

          'I, the undersigned, herewith report my
     withdrawal from your organization and I am asking
     you to take immediate notice of this. While I am
     asking you to strike my name from your membership
     list, I am also sending you my best wishes for the
     success of your organization. I regret that
     personal interests have forced me to dissolve my
     connection with your organization. As proof that I
     have sent you this declaration, I am retaining a
     copy of it . . . '
     "This scrap of paper was signed by the workers of

the firm Kuh, Nathan and Fischer as well as Hirsch, Elton and Co. and sent to the union. Now the manufacturers may do what they want. They will certainly take advantage of their victory.

"There are a number of reasons why the Socialist Labor party has so far made little progress here, the chief of which is the lower middle class' fight for survival. For those who merely observe the surface of things, all the fuss about free silver coinage must remain totally incomprehensible or be viewed as a battle between the gold and silver interests. Here in the West this demand is only a symbol, a banner (if I may be permitted to use such a daring image) around which the petit-bourgeoisie (among them many workers who own land and house) rallies while facing perdition. They run around in fear like chickens with their heads cut off. Suddenly they discover the faint silver light and rush upon it from all sides in the belief that salvation beckons. A horrendous disappointment is bound to come. But at the moment, everybody in the West is in favor of silver. I say 'everybody' because the number of actual proletarians is relatively small and, having not yet gathered in class-conscious organizations, they are lacking a comprehension of the situation. It is no wonder that the majority of them are currently also raving about silver. Many of them (in Illinois) are saying: 'Oh well, I don't care if it's gold or silver but I am for Altgeld.' No doubt, Altgeld is not only a strange but also a significant man, an organizer without equal. When he freed the Anarchists three years ago, there was the unanimous opinion that he had become a political liability. He could not have cared less about all of this fuss, and he continued to do things which were unheard of for a politician. His behavior towards Cleveland, his exposure of prominent tax evaders, his fight against the big newspapers (all of them are against him), and many of his other acts were so unusual for a politician that it was assumed that he had committed political suicide. But it was exactly these actions which won him the sympathy of the masses, so that he is today the absolute ruler over the Democratic Party of Illinois. Not only did his party unanimously re-elect him as its candidate, it also incorporated into the party platform all of the resolutions that he espoused. His enemies now assert that he was only able to do so by crafty stratagems. That this is not so was proven by an assembly convoked by his foes in the Auditorium (a gigantic hall in Chicago). Even though the party bigwigs had been mobilized and the big department stores had urged their employees to attend this assembly, it was poorly attended and the upper galleries remained closed. Those that attended hissed when one of the orators attacked Altgeld. Of course the cause that he represents, that of the silver barons, is

rotten. But what must not be disregarded is the fact
that the masses fight for this cause with entirely new
tactics. I am referring to the vehement attacks upon
big capital and the bitterness which is welling up--so
contrary to the aims of the politicians. The enthusiasm
for silver will fade, but the hatred for big capital
will remain. As far as the masses are concerned, we are
facing here a 'socialism for the stupid people.' Dire
need has brought forth this movement. The need will
remain and discover other cures. To mention this only:
in Wisconsin a bushel of potatoes went for 4 and 5 and
even 1 cent. Stores are hoarding everywhere and the
reserve army of labor is swelling tremendously. I know
very well that the Democratic politicians would like to
forget the unpleasant question: 'tariffs or free
trade?' but the eagerness with which the new bait was
swallowed in the West shows that the hunger for
salvation is mighty.

"Just how much the silver intoxication has spread,
may be illustrated by the fact that the Socialist Labor
Party not long ago refused to take a decisive position
in this question. Some of the members of the party
might have been encouraged in this attitude by the
circumstances that the proponents of gold currency are
the real big capitalists. The real socialists find it
very difficult to be without a newspaper that fights for
their principles. Several weeks ago, an editor of the
Arbeiterzeitung attempted to prove to the workers that
it would be a misfortune for them to strike for a wage
increase (his argument was that a strike would increase
the production costs). He did not get very far with
this argument. The same newspaper praised the
'lumpenproletariat' exuberantly for awhile. It spoke
literally of 'the brothers in the penitentiary' which
did not prevent, however, the paper from attacking the
police on a daily basis (and it will do so in the
future) because they were not protecting property and
life, i.e., the police were not putting the 'brothers'
or the 'fifth estate' fast enough into the penitentiary.
Such a situation cannot last and sooner or later a
change will occur.

"The Anarchist movement is not stirring at the
moment. But the Socialist Labor Party, too, has made no
progress and the trade unions are also doing badly. The
Socialist Trade and Labor Alliance so far meets with
little enthusiasm. Nevertheless, wherever one looks one
sees ferment and new forces forming. As far as Chicago
is concerned, there cannot be a successful Socialist
agitation until the silver movement has collapsed. But
then the sky is the limit."

Quod felix faustumque sit!

Chapter XV: Endnotes

[1]It should be pointed out here that the quotations have been taken verbatim et punctuatim from the official organ."

[2]Because of the interminable squabbles among the Jewish organizations.

[3]These words are taken from the Declaration of Independence of July 4th, 1776.

Index

About the Translator

KAI SCHOENHALS is Associate Professor of History at Kenyon College, Ohio. His earlier works include *Revolution and Intervention in Grenada,* the *Collected Works of Marx and Engels,* Volume 5 (translation), and various articles published in the *Caribbean Review.*